UN SECURITY COUNCIL RESOLUTION 242:
THE BUILDING BLOCK OF PEACEMAKING

CONTRIBUTORS ADNAN ABU ODEH
NABIL ELARABY
MEIR ROSENNE
DENNIS ROSS
EUGENE ROSTOW
VERNON TURNER

On the occasion of the 25th anniversary of UN Resolution 242

A WASHINGTON INSTITUTE MONOGRAPH

Library of Congress Cataloging-in-Publication Data

UN Security Council resolution 242: the building block of peacemaking: proceedings from the Washington Institute's Harris Symposium/ Featuring addresses by Eugene V. Rostow ... [et al.] and a supplementary document section.
    p.   cm.
"A Washington Institute monograph"
ISBN 0-944-029-51-5
1. Jewish-Arab relations—Congresses. 2. Israel-Arab War, 1967- —Influence—Congresses. 3. United Nations—Palestine—Congresses. I. Rostow, Eugene V. (Eugene Victor), 1913- . II. Washington Institute for Near East Policy. III. Title: United Nations Security Council resolution 242.
DS119.7.U48 1993
327.5694017'4927--dc20   93-18860
                                                   CIP

Copyright © 1993 by
The Washington Institute for Near East Policy
1828 L Street, N.W., Suite 1050
Washington, D.C. 20036
Library of Congress Catalog Card Number: 93-18860
ISBN 0-944029-51-5

Cover Design by Jill Indyk

CONTENTS

Preface	v
Contributors	vii
Introduction	1
PART I: The Intent of UNSC 242—The View of Non-Regional Actors **Eugene Rostow** **Vernon Turner**	5
PART II Legal Interpretations of UNSC 242 **Meir Rosenne** **Nabil Elaraby**	31
PART III The Origins and Relevance of UNSC 242 **Adnan Abu Odeh**	47
PART IV UNSC 242 and Arab-Israeli Peacemaking **Dennis Ross**	61
SUPPLEMENTARY DOCUMENTS	73

CONTRIBUTORS

Adnan Abu Odeh has served since March 1992 as the Permanent Representative of Jordan to the United Nations, following two decades of personal service to His Majesty King Hussein. During that time, he held positions as Chief of the Royal Court, Political Advisor to the King, Minister of Court, and Secretary-General of the National Union of Jordan. In addition, he has served in various Jordanian governments as Minister of Information and Culture and Minister of Occupied Territories Affairs. A former Fellow at Harvard University's Center for International Affairs, Ambassador Abu Odeh is the author of "An Undivided Jerusalem" (*Foreign Affairs*, Spring 1992).

Nabil Elaraby has served as the Permanent Representative of Egypt to the United Nations since August 1991. An expert in international law, Ambassador Elaraby completed two tours of duty as director of the Legal and Treaties Department of the Egyptian Foreign Ministry (1976-1978, 1983-1987). In addition, he was Egypt's ambassador to India from 1981 to 1983. Intimately involved in legal aspects of peacemaking since 1973, Ambassador Elaraby served as legal advisor to Egypt's delegation to the Geneva Peace Conference and to the Camp David negotiations as well as head of Egypt's delegation to the Taba talks.

Meir Rosenne served as legal advisor to Israel's Foreign Ministry from 1971-1979, actively participating in Arab-Israeli negotiations from the Kilometer 101 talks to the Israel-Egypt Peace Treaty. He was head of the Israeli team to the autonomy talks until September 1979, when he was appointed ambassador to France and, subsequently, ambassador to the United States. Ambassador Rosenne, who holds a doctorate in international law from the Sorbonne, currently serves as president and chief executive officer of the State of Israel Bonds Organization.

Dennis B. Ross, special advisor on the Middle East to Secretary of State Warren Christopher, served in the Bush administration as Director of the State Department's Policy Planning Staff and as assistant to the president for policy planning. He has previously served as director of Near East and South Asian Affairs on the National Security Council staff and as deputy director of the Pentagon's Office of Net Assessment. A former Senior Fellow of The Washington Institute, Ambassador Ross also served as Executive Director of the Berkeley-Stanford Program on Soviet International Behavior.

Eugene V. Rostow, the Sterling Professor of Law and Public Affairs at Yale Law School, served as undersecretary of state for political affairs from 1966 to 1969, during which time he was a central figure in the diplomacy surrounding the passage of UNSC 242. A professor at Yale Law School since 1938, he served as its dean from 1955 to 1965. He has also held positions as director of the Arms Control and Disarmament Agency, Distinguished Research Professor at the National Defense University, and Distinguished Fellow at the United States Institute of Peace. A noted legal scholar, his published works include *Law, Power and the Pursuit of Peace* (1968), *Peace in the Balance* (1972), and *The Ideal in Law* (1978).

Vernon Turner was counsellor for political affairs to Canada's delegation to the United Nations from 1964 to 1969, and, during Canada's two-year term in the Security Council (1967-1969), was charged with special responsibility for the Middle East. He later went on to serve as Ambassador to Israel (1982-1986) and then to the Soviet Union (1986-1990). Though he retired from the diplomatic corps in 1991, Ambassador Turner continues to serve as special advisor to the Canadian Foreign Ministry's Task Force on Central and Eastern Europe.

PREFACE

Ever since its adoption by the United Nations Security Council on November 22, 1967, Resolution 242 has provided context for peacemaking efforts between Arabs and Israelis. It was the basis for the only peace treaty ever signed between Israel and an Arab country, Egypt, in 1979, and the foundation for the current peace talks launched by the Madrid peace conference in October 1991. After twenty-five years, the critical elements of the resolution—peace, security and land—are still the main issues of contention between the parties to the peace talks.

For this reason, The Washington Institute took the occasion of the twenty-fifth anniversary of the resolution's passage to devote its 1992 Harris Symposium to examine anew the framework for peacemaking enunciated in the resolution, and especially the meaning of the three central issues of peace, security and land. The Symposium addressed the original intent of the resolution's drafters; the various, often conflicting, legal interpretations of the resolution's twin calls for territorial withdrawal and the establishment of "secure and recognized boundaries"; and the relevance of the resolution for the current negotiations.

This volume contains the presentations of six diplomats and legal scholars—Adnan Abu Odeh, Nabil Elaraby, Meir Rosenne, Dennis Ross, Eugene Rostow, and Vernon Turner. Together, this distinguished group spans the last quarter-century of peacemaking, including diplomats who represented their respective governments during the negotiations over the final wording of the resolution, veterans of Camp David, a senior political advisor to Jordan's King Hussein, and an American diplomat who was instrumental to the convening of the current peace talks launched at Madrid.

Of special significance in this volume is the supplementary document section which contains several early drafts of the resolution. These drafts help shed light on the attitude of various members of the Security Council prior to the adoption of the ultimate version of UNSC 242. Included as well is a collection of statements by various U.S. officials and legal interpretations by several international legal experts on the importance of UNSC 242.

Today, more than twenty-five years after the adoption of UNSC 242, it is our hope that this volume will contribute to a better understanding of the resolution as the parties continue their negotiations in an effort to reach a just, comprehensive and lasting peace in the Middle East.

Barbi Weinberg
President
April 1993

INTRODUCTION

Twenty-five years after its adoption in the aftermath of the Six Day War on November 22, 1967, United Nations Security Council Resolution 242 [hereafter UNSC 242] is still the essential reference point for the Arab-Israeli peace process and a building block for peacemaking. One reason why the resolution has held such a central position in efforts to promote peace in the Middle East is that it is open to several different interpretations; the resolution's ambiguities—specifically the extent of Israeli withdrawal from the occupied territories, and the nature of peace and security in the region—are indeed the points of contention between the Arabs and Israel in the current negotiations. This collection of studies marking the twenty-fifth anniversary of the resolution's adoption stems from The Washington Institute's Harris Symposium, which sought to address the continuing importance of UNSC 242 to the peace process.

In Part I of this Monograph, Eugene Rostow and Vernon Turner, both intimately involved in the Security Council debate over the wording of UNSC 242, discuss their understanding of the original intent of the resolution. Eugene Rostow argues that from America's perspective, UNSC 242 was meant to provide a fair basis for a fair peace. Its intent was not to force Israel back to the fragile and vulnerable armistice demarcation lines, but rather to provide a basis for negotiations in which the parties themselves would establish the exact boundaries. The omission of the definite article "the" before the word "territories" was deliberate and intended to leave open the possibility of modifications to the pre-1967 lines in the final settlement.

Vernon Turner relates that the text of UNSC 242 was the product of many minds and many pens. The key elements

2/ UNSC 242: The Building Block of Peacemaking

had existed since the Six Day War: withdrawal of forces, termination of belligerence, freedom of transit through international waterways, solution of the refugee problem, peaceful settlement of the conflict, and the appointment of a UN special representative to help achieve these goals. For several months, the members of the Security Council, along with other interested parties in the General Assembly, grappled with various drafts that sought to relate Israel's withdrawal from occupied territory to the other elements of an overall settlement. In the end, Britain's Lord Caradon was able to produce a draft resolution that took into account Israel's security needs and the Arabs' desire for withdrawal. At the last minute, the Soviets attempted to clarify the Resolution by inserting the word "all" before the word "territories," and even tabled their own draft resolution, but they failed. Instead, UNSC 242 included the intentionally ambiguous call for Israeli "withdrawal... from territories," balanced with the declared right of all states in the area to live in peace within "secure and recognized boundaries."

Part II focuses on the legal ramifications of UNSC 242 as interpreted by Meir Rosenne and Nabil Elaraby, both legal scholars as well as veterans of the peace negotiations between Israel and Egypt. In Meir Rosenne's view, UNSC 242 was originally written to deal with the acquisition of territory, not its occupation, and remains the basis for a peace settlement between Israel and Arab states in the Middle East. However, it must be remembered that UNSC 242 applies specifically to the "states concerned" still in a state of war with Israel, and therefore does not include the Palestinians, who are not a state. The historical record indicates that the word "withdrawal" was not intended to force a withdrawal from all the territories. Rather, UNSC 242 requires that the parties negotiate in good faith in order to reach several outcomes: withdrawal of Israeli forces to secure and recognized boundaries established by mutual agreement; termination of belligerent actions against Israel, including an economic boycott; and the recognition by all parties of each other's independence and statehood.

Nabil Elaraby stresses three important aspects of the resolution: first, that it was adopted unanimously; second, that it has been re-confirmed by the Security Council in other resolutions, notably UNSC 338; and third, that it has been applied only once, during the Camp David talks. Since UNSC 242 was not a privately negotiated document, but rather adopted in accordance with the UN Charter, the principles of international law are more pertinent than the interpretations of any of the drafters in determining how to apply the resolution to Arab-Israeli peacemaking. Under international law as dictated by the Vienna Convention on the Law of Treaties, the acquisition of territory is disavowed; thus Ambassador Elaraby contends that it is a myth that the omission of the definite article "the" in the English draft condones the acquisition of territory through the use of force. The reference to "secure and recognized boundaries" in the resolution should be understood only in the context of the end of belligerency and the establishment of conditions for peace, and not as a stipulation that the boundaries be redrawn.

Adnan Abu Odeh, in Part III, discusses the continuing relevance of UNSC 242. According to Abu Odeh, UNSC 242's viability and tenacity, as reflected in both its spirit and letter, has enabled it to become a blueprint for peace in the Middle East. The spirit of the resolution is that peace and territorial acquisition by force are incompatible. The letter requires withdrawal, on the one hand, and recognition and security, on the other. Because of the balanced nature of the text, as well as its inherent ambiguity, UNSC 242 can serve as a framework for peace negotiations. The Arab acceptance of UNSC 242 established a trend towards peacemaking in which the recognition of the state of Israel was an essential element of the whole. Before UNSC 242, Arab states felt that peace was impossible as long as the state of Israel existed; thus, the passage of UNSC 242 changed the Arab-Israeli conflict from one between competing nationalisms to a dispute over territory. The drafters of UNSC 242 did not foresee the long duration of the Israeli occupation of the West Bank and Gaza Strip, which has served to focus Palestinian grievances and promote the emergence of an independent Palestinian actor, but it has been able to adapt to this new reality. UNSC 242 is still very relevant today, twenty-five years after its adoption.

In Part IV, Dennis Ross, a key member of the American team that worked to launch the peace talks that began with the Madrid conference, addresses the role of UNSC 242 in the peace process. UNSC 242, he states, has been embraced as a reference point by all of the parties, and has been at the core of every important peacemaking effort in the region. Its durability proves that there must be something right about it. Although UNSC 242 is a clear reference point, the ambiguity in its terms and meaning made the road to Madrid a difficult one. The United States has tried not to interpret the resolution itself, so as to not prejudice the negotiations, but rather to leave it to the parties themselves to resolve any ambiguity.

This examination of the relevance of a historical document to current peace negotiations is a valuable tool for diplomats, policymakers, and historians alike. In addition to edited presentations described above, this volume also contains an extensive document section which traces the resolution's origins, its implementation, and its continuing value as a reference point in the peace process twenty-five years after its adoption.

PART I

THE INTENT OF UNSC RESOLUTION 242—THE VIEW OF NON-REGIONAL ACTORS

Eugene Rostow

This meeting is intended to take note of the fact that the UNSC 242 is twenty-five years old. There seems to be a good deal of doubt in various capitals of the world as to whether we should celebrate the anniversary or don mourning for the occasion. The Western nations doggedly repeat that peace negotiations between Israel and the Arab states must be based on UNSC 242 and UNSC 338, which makes UNSC 242 legally binding under Article 25 of the UN Charter. UNSC 338 commands the parties to start "immediately, and concurrently with the cease-fire," in order to establish a just and durable peace "in accordance with the terms of Resolution 242."

Spokesmen for the Western allies do not always interpret UNSC 242 in exactly the same way, however. The Arab nations, with the notable exception of Egypt, claim somewhat inconsistently, that UNSC 242 is hopelessly ambiguous, and also that it clearly means the opposite of what its language was universally understood to mean when it was debated, negotiated, and adopted. It is not yet clear whether Russia and the other successor states to the Soviet Union have abandoned the pre-Gorbachev Soviet position on UNSC 242, which was identical to that of the Arabs.

While most Israelis agree that Israel should continue to pursue the goal of formal peace with its neighbors, even at a comparatively high price in territorial concessions, an increasing number of Israelis doubt whether any Arabs are willing to follow Egyptian President Anwar Sadat's example by making peace on terms compatible with both Security Council resolutions. Therefore, they argue, Israel should be content with the status quo established by the 1949 Armistice Agreement as modified by the Egyptian-Israeli peace treaty: that is, that Israel should continue to occupy the West Bank, the Gaza Strip and the Golan Heights. In view of the increasing slaughter of Arabs by other Arabs in the West Bank and the Gaza Strip, there is an increase also in the number of Israelis willing to consider massive expulsions of Palestinian-Arabs from the occupied territories.

If the Middle East peace process survives the next few months, there is a further reason for the diplomats to stick closely to the twin resolutions, 242 and 338: they are the only documents setting out principles for peace-keeping on which Israel, its Arab neighbors, and the Security Council have formally agreed. They were the basis for the successful peace between Israel and Egypt in 1979, and there is little possibility that the parties in the Security Council could reach agreement on a substitute agenda.

I should make my own position clear. I remain of the opinion that UNSC 242 was a wise judgment when it was negotiated and voted in 1967, and that it still provides a fair basis for a fair peace if the parties apply the twin resolutions in strict conformity with their terms. Moreover, the condition of world politics today ought to favor a general peace between Israel and the Arab states. In the aftermath of the collapse of the Soviet Union, Russia, China, India, and the East European states and most of the successor states of the former Soviet Union have established diplomatic relations with Israel. Jordan has recently indicated that it is seriously considering the same course, and even Syria seems to be moving in the same direction. And this trend, this highly desirable and promising trend, leaves the Arab population of the West Bank and the Gaza Strip (often wrongly called "The Palestinians") more and more isolated politically. There will, in my opinion, never be a more propitious time for the Palestinian Arabs of the West Bank and the Gaza Strip to make peace.

Indeed, a serious Israeli commentator, Jon Kimche, has concluded that the continuing presence of UNSC 242 as a source of reference has become a major obstacle to peace negotiations in the vastly changed political climate of 1992. He writes that UNSC 242

> provides a convenient alibi for all who do not want peace. UNSC 242 was cobbled together in 1967 as a stop-gap to prevent the UN from doing something silly in the wake of the Six Day War. It served its purpose then. It has done its duty. It should now be allowed to rest in peace and obscurity like so many other resolutions. The prospect for peace in 1992 and 1993 is too real to allow it to be further blocked by the ghost of UNSC 242. There should now be an international ban on all further reference to this outdated symbol of UN indecision.[1]

Before addressing the role of the non-regional actors in the negotiations which led to UNSC 242, we should recall the circumstances which produced the Six Day War, for those circumstances profoundly affected the terms of the agreement which was embodied in UNSC 242.

It is often said that the Six Day War was brought about by accident or a miscalculation or by mutual misunderstanding. This is not the case. The Six Day War was brought on by Arab (particularly Syrian and Egyptian) aggression deliberately incited by the Soviet Union. A CIA cable, recently declassified in sanitized form, sums up the situation as the United States and the Western Allies experienced it every day during the late spring of 1967. This cable reports a conversation between a CIA officer and a "medium-level Soviet official." The Soviet official told

---

[1] Jon Kimche, "Arab-Israeli Peace—The End of Resolution 242", 38 *Midstream*, No. 8, November, 1992, 1, 6.

his interlocutor that there had been "miscalculations" by the Soviets and by the Arabs:

> The Soviets overestimated the Arabs' ability to employ their substantial military strength against the Israelis, while the Arabs overrated their own strength and underrated the Israeli military capability and determination to win. When the source asked if that meant that the Soviets had encouraged the Arabs in their hostile attitude towards Israel, the Soviet replied affirmatively, stating that the USSR had wanted to create another trouble spot for the United States in addition to that already existing in Vietnam. The Soviet aim was to create a situation in which the United States would become seriously involved economically, politically, and possibly even militarily, and in which the United States would suffer serious political reverses as a result of its siding against the Arabs.

This grand design, which envisaged a long war in the Middle East, misfired because the Arabs failed completely and the Israeli blitzkrieg was so decisive. Faced with this situation, the Soviets had no alternative but to back down as quickly and as gracefully as possible so as not to appear the villains of the conflict.

> The Soviet thought Nasser 'must go' and that he would 'most probably' be assassinated in the near future by his own disillusioned people. He said that Nasser's charge that U.S. and British aircraft had aided the Israeli forces was a desperate attempt to save face in the Arab world after suffering a humiliating military defeat and that no one, certainly not the USSR, believes the charge. In a final comment, the Soviet said 'The war has

shown that the Arabs are incapable of unity when their vital interest are at stake.'[1]

Apart from supplying arms and military advisers to the Arabs on a large scale, the Soviet incitement to the war consisted mainly of the deliberate dissemination of false intelligence. Given the emotional intensity of the Arabs' sense of grievance about the existence of Israel, the Soviet program of disinformation was the equivalent of throwing gasoline on a fire.

There had been active friction between Syria and Israel since September 1966, focused largely on water rights and guerrilla activities. The United States was host to an international conference on Water for Peace scheduled to convene in Washington at the end of May, 1967. In order to calm the situation and head off possible Israeli retaliation against Syria, the United States sought a Security Council resolution directed against Syria. Negotiations at the UN in New York produced what the United States thought was a Soviet-American agreement on a compromise resolution so watered down that the criticism of Syria was almost invisible. The Soviet permanent representative at the Security Council then vetoed the resolution we believed he had promised to support.

I have often wondered in retrospect whether it was a mistake for the United States to have invested so much time and effort in a Security Council resolution. A sharp Israeli attack on Syria in the fall of 1966 might well have been a more effective deterrent than the pitiful fiasco in the Security Council.

One of the most important factors in the coming of the war was the development of a feverish conviction among the Arab states that their armies could defeat the Israelis and thus avenge their defeats in 1948 and 1949, which they

---

[1] Released by the Lyndon B. Johnson Library, Austin, Texas, Document No. 84 li, Case No. 82-156, May 3, 1984.

excused because of their faulty intelligence about Israeli capabilities, and in 1956, which they blamed on British and French participation.

From September 1966, when I joined the State Department, until the outbreak of war in June 1967, the situation became more and more threatening, as attacks on Israel, largely from Syria and Jordan, increased in number and severity, and the Israeli countermoves against those attacks increased correspondingly. During the spring of 1967, the Soviet Union began to spread false reports that Israel was planning to attack Syria and that it had mobilized twelve or fourteen brigades near the Golan Heights for that purpose. There was no truth in these reports, as we knew from our own military attaches and the reports of the UN forces then in Israel, but the Soviets kept repeating these charges with emphasis and urgency, not simply as rumors to be spread in bazaars, but as formal diplomatic demarche to Egypt and other Arab countries, and to Israel. Israel even offered to take the Soviet ambassador to Israel on an inspection trip of the area, but he refused.

The Soviet program of disinformation began to have far-reaching effects. Arab radio stations and newspapers taunted President Nasser. "You claim to be the big brother of the Arab people," the Arab voices said, "but Israel is about to bash Syria, and you are doing nothing." Sensitive to such criticism since it touched his pan-Arab nerve, Nasser responded not only with great rhetorical vigor but also with what soon became a mobilization. First he promised to fight if Syria were attacked. These cries soon merged, however, with broader promises to lead a holy war against Israel and to throw the Israelis "into the sea." Soon Arab troops from Algeria and Iraq joined Egyptian, Syrian, Saudi and Jordanian forces in a ring around Israel.

As the threat of another Arab war against Israel became obvious during the early spring of 1967, the United States, Great Britain and their allies undertook active diplomatic steps to resolve what was more and more visibly a crisis.

The American reaction to the course of events was a classic demonstration of the diplomatic style of President Johnson and Secretary of State Rusk. That style was characterized by careful preparation and a long-term perspective and involved sustained and energetic consultations with everybody affected or involved. It was common for President Johnson, discussing a proposal from the bureaucracy, to ask, "If we do what you recommend, where will we be in twenty years? Let's think it over and meet again on Friday."

Both Rusk and Johnson had had a great deal of experience with Middle Eastern questions, Rusk as Assistant Secretary of State in the Truman administration, Johnson as Democratic Majority Leader and Chairman of the Senate Armed Services Committee during the Eisenhower years. Johnson had played an active and important role in the diplomatic settlement after the Suez War of 1956.

A high-level "Control Committee" was set up within the United States government at the undersecretary level to consider, prepare and propose policies the United States and its allies might pursue in concert, both in the UN forum and independently, if necessary. A special committee was appointed, under the chairmanship of Ambassador Julius Holmes, to appraise Soviet policy toward the Middle East. Its conclusion was that the purpose of the Soviet drive in the Middle East was to exploit Arab hostility to the existence of Israel as a weapon which could enable them not only to gain control of the oil reserves of the area but also to outflank NATO from the south and thus neutralize Western Europe. Checking the Soviet goal in the Middle East would require a vigorous American and allied diplomacy and military presence and support for Israel, Iran and Saudi Arabia.

In order to understand the political context of UNSC 242, it is also necessary to recall the international atmosphere of the time. The Vietnam War was militarily at a dismal point, and was beginning to poison American domestic politics and the relationship of the United States with its allies as well. The relationship among the NATO allies was still bleeding from the wounds inflicted by U.S. policy during the Suez crisis of 1956. De Gaulle was pursuing a policy of pique toward the United States, as he struggled to restore French pride in the aftermath of Algeria, Suez, and Indochina. The Six Day War occurred less than a year after General de Gaulle ordered the NATO forces out of France and Belgium stepped forward to receive the NATO headquarters on its soil.

Nevertheless, President Johnson and Secretary Rusk launched an extremely active and far-reaching Middle Eastern policy initiative based on the assumption that NATO solidarity could be achieved and maintained as the solid nucleus of a much larger coalition extending around the world.

In the period before the Six Day War broke out, high-level officials from Washington frequently visited the capitals of key countries and the North Atlantic Council in order to pursue extended consultations. The British and American Middle Eastern teams met regularly both in London and in Washington to examine the available policy alternatives, and to recommend policy goals that would command general support outside what was then still the Soviet bloc and the Arab world. The United States was in nearly constant communication, also, with the governments of Israel, Egypt, and the Soviet Union.

There were several objectives of these exhaustive consultations: to explore every possible way to cool the growing crisis; to prevent a war in which the Soviet Union might decide to intervene; to clarify the goals of American policy toward the region; and to reach agreement on a policy for the future of the Middle East that could be supported by as large a majority as possible in the UN. In President Johnson's view, America's first goal in the area was to prevent what became the Six Day War, to face down possible Soviet intervention without provoking it, to promote NATO solidarity in every possible way, and to push the Arabs toward peace after twenty years of intransigent resistance to the idea of peace with Israel. I believe that these consultations, coupled with the universal perceptions of Soviet, Syrian, and Egyptian aggression, permitted the U.S. and Great Britain, acting together, to achieve something close to unanimity among the Western allies, and, on that basis, to obtain the passage of UNSC 242, the only time since 1947 that the Western bloc has agreed about how to handle an episode in the long Arab war against Israel.

While these efforts were being pursued, Nasser requested the UN peacekeeping force to withdraw from the frontier between Israel and Egypt, including Sharm el Sheik at the mouth of the Straits of Tiran. U Thant, the Secretary-General of the UN at that time, replied that if Nasser wished the UN peacekeeping forces to withdraw from part of the area they were patrolling, he would have to ask those troops to withdraw from the entire frontier. By prior agreement with Nasser, the Indian and Yugoslav troops, which were part of the UN force, withdrew immediately, thus destroying the force as a potential obstacle to war, however fragile.

President Johnson forcefully denounced the Egyptian move for two reasons: first, the withdrawal of the UN forces in itself greatly increased the risk of war; and second, it had been agreed by the parties in 1957, as part of the price for Israeli withdrawal from the Sinai, that any use of force by Egypt to close the Straits of Tiran would be treated as an armed attack, not only by the Israelis, but also by Great Britain and the U.S., who had negotiated the agreement between Israel and Egypt, and guaranteed the Straits as an international waterway. That agreement provided for a special procedure of delay to be followed if Egypt ever did try to close the Straits of Tiran.

When the Egyptian troops manned the guns controlling the Straits and announced that the waterway was closed to Israeli shipping, the first shot in the Six Day War had been fired. It is no wonder that, in a major speech on June 19,

President Johnson said, "If a single act of folly was more responsible for this explosion than any other, I think it was the arbitrary and dangerous announced decision that the Straits of Tiran would be closed. The right of innocent maritime passage must be preserved for all nations."[1]

The period between May 23, when the Straits were closed, and June 5 was one of frantic diplomatic effort by the United States, its allies, and many other friendly countries around the world to defuse the crisis by persuading Nasser to restore the situation in the Sinai as it had been before the dissolution of the UN peacekeeping force. That campaign was supplemented by a determined effort to organize an allied naval force to escort Israeli and other vessels through the Straits of Tiran. The idea was suggested by the British government, and was embraced as a matter of extreme urgency by Johnson and Rusk. Former President Eisenhower confirmed to Johnson that he had indeed guaranteed the Straits of Tiran and assured Johnson of his full support, "as a matter of national honor," if Johnson decided to use force.[2]

In view of the controversy then raging in Congress over the Vietnam War, it was deemed politic to obtain a congressional resolution specifically supporting military action to break the blockade of the Straits of Tiran. The U.S., the Netherlands, Canada, and Australia quickly rallied to the British plan and prepared to carry out the task. When Secretary of State Rusk and Secretary of Defense Robert McNamara consulted congressional leaders on the subject, however, they found great reluctance to

---

[1] Public Papers of the Presidents, Lyndon B. Johnson, Book 1, No. 272, 630, 633.

[2] Legal Aspects of the Search for Peace in the Middle East, Address before the Sixty-Fourth Annual Meeting of the American Society for International Law (April 24, 1970), in *American Journal of International Law* [AJIL] 64, pp. 65-71 (1970). See Section D in the document section at the rear of this book.

authorize "another Vietnam," and a great preference to support an Israeli action in self-defense. When Jordan put its armed forces under Egyptian control, Johnson concluded that war was inevitable. It would have been unconscionable for the U.S. to press Israel to delay any further in recourse to its legal rights of self-defense.

The difference of opinion between Congress and the President was never resolved. As the Arab mobilization reached a climax, the war exploded. The Soviet Union, which had resisted American proposals for a cease-fire for days, suddenly changed its mind as the Arab armies surrendered and the Israelis reached the Suez Canal.

The long months of study and diplomacy devoted to the Middle Eastern crisis of 1966 and 1967 produced a prompt articulation of Anglo-American policy after the Six Day War. President Johnson's speech of June 19 pronounced the ideas which were eventually incorporated into UNSC 242 after four more months of heated debate in the Security Council, the General Assembly, and then the Security Council again.

Johnson's June 19 speech makes seven principal points that were to become the essence of UNSC 242:

(1) Israel should not have to withdraw its forces to the pre-June 5 armistice lines. "This is not a prescription for peace," the president said, "but for a renewal of hostilities." Of course, that was the policy adopted in 1957 when the Israelis withdrew from the Sinai without any peace treaty and it was widely felt throughout the allied governments that that was a mistake never to be repeated.

(2) There must be peace between the parties, real peace, before there could be any troop withdrawal. This principle, not spelled out in detail in the June 19 speech, was fully discussed before the UN. It reflected the history of the 1957 agreement, which settled the Suez War of 1956 and required Israel to withdraw from the Sinai in exchange for a series of promises by Egypt, all of which were broken: to respect Israel's borders; to allow Israel free passage in the international waterways of the region; and to make peace.

More than any other factor, the Egyptian breach of the 1957 agreement led to the basic requirement of UNSC 242 that Israel could remain in the occupied territories until the parties established "a just and lasting peace in the Middle East." Secretary Rusk was a particularly strong advocate of this position because of Egypt's violation of the 1957 agreement. The correlative principle of UNSC 242, that the new and secure boundaries of Israel need not be the same as the Armistice Demarcation Lines of 1949, simply echo the terms of the Armistice Agreements themselves, which provide that the Armistice Lines are not to be considered political boundaries, but can be changed when the parties move from armistice to peace.

(3) Peace agreements must be negotiated by the parties. "It's hard to see," the President said, "how nations can live together in peace if they cannot learn to reason together. The nations of the region have had only fragile and violated truce lines for twenty years. What they need now are recognized boundaries and other arrangements that will give security against terror, destruction and war."

(4) All the states in the region have the same right to have their territorial integrity and political independence respected. Threats to destroy any one nation have become a burden to the peace.

(5) There must be justice for the refugees.

(6) Maritime rights through international waterways in the area must be respected.

(7) The special interests of the three great religions in Jerusalem must also be assured.

Two of these issues have proved to be especially critical in the diplomacy of obtaining the passage of the resolution in 1967 and in the subsequent struggle to implement it: first, the issue of coupling Israeli withdrawals and agreements on the establishment of a state of peace, and second, the question of how much withdrawal and whether Israel is required by the resolution to withdraw to the Armistice Demarcation Lines of 1949.

Since UNSC 242 calls on Israel to withdraw only from territories occupied in the course of the Six Day War—that is, not from *all* the territories or even from *the* territories it occupied in the course of the war—and since most of the boundaries in question are no more than armistice lines specifically designated as *not* being political boundaries, it is hard to believe that professional diplomats can seriously claim in 1992 that UNSC 242 requires Israel to return to the 1967 Armistice Lines. This Arab position is particularly bizarre applied to the West Bank and the Gaza Strip, where, under the Mandate and Article 80 of the UN Charter, the Jewish people still have an incontestably valid claim to make close settlements on the land.

Five and a half months of vehement public diplomacy in 1967 make the meaning of the missing definite article in UNSC 242 perfectly clear. Ingeniously drafted resolutions calling for withdrawal from *all* the territory were defeated in the Security Council and the General Assembly one after another. Speaker after speaker made it explicit that Israel was not to be forced back to the "fragile and vulnerable" Armistice Demarcation Lines but should retire, once peace was made, to what UNSC 242 called "secure and recognized" boundaries agreed to by the parties. In negotiating such agreements, the parties should take into account, among other factors, security considerations, assured access to the international waterways of the region, a just settlement of the refugee problem, and, of course, their respective legal claims.

In 1967, Lawrence Hargrove, the director of the American Society of International Law, was senior adviser on international law to the United States Mission to the UN. In 1971, in testimony before a Subcommittee of the House Committee on Foreign Affairs, he said:

> The language "from territories" was regarded at the time of the adoption of the resolution as of high consequence because the proposal put forward by those espousing the Egyptian case was

withdrawal from "the" territories. In the somewhat minute debate which frequently characterizes the period before the adoption of a United Nations resolution, the article "the" was regarded of considerable significance because its inclusion would seem to imply withdrawal from all territories which Israel had not occupied prior to the June war but was at the present time occupying.

Consequently, the omission of "the" was intended on our part, as I understood it at the time and it was understood at all sides, to leave open the possibility of modifications in the lines which were occupied as of June 4, 1967 in the final settlement.[1]

In the case of Egypt, Israel accepted an agreement without territorial change as sufficient to satisfy UNSC 242. It provides *inter alia* for the demilitarization and international protection of the Sinai Desert. The Sinai Desert, occupied by Israel between 1967 and 1979, had been Egyptian territory and was never part of the Mandate.

The Egyptian model fits neither the Jordanian nor the Syrian case, however. Israel has a better legal claim to the West Bank than Jordan, and every military group which has studied the problem agrees that Israeli security requires control of the high places of the West Bank of the Jordan River, at least. In the case of the Golan Heights, former Secretary of Defense McNamara has said that if he were the Israel's Minister of Defense, he would never agree to giving up the Golan Heights.

In short, UNSC 242 authorizes the parties to make whatever territorial changes the situation requires—it does not require the Israelis to transfer to the Arabs all,

---

[1] U.S. Congress, House of Representatives, Hearings before the Subcommittee on the Middle East of the Committee on Foreign Affairs, April, 1971.

most, or indeed any of the occupied territories. The Egyptian-Israeli peace treaty awards to an Arab state more than 90 percent of the territory Israel captured in the Six Day War. Can anyone say with a straight face that UNSC 242 requires the transfer of occupied territory in the West Bank and the Golan Heights, as well? It surely permits such a transfer if the parties accept it, but it does not require it.

It is quite true that during the negotiations leading to the adoption of UNSC 242, some American representatives said that the resolution contemplated only minor changes in the Armistice Demarcation Lines between Israel and Jordan as the parties with drew to a permanent boundary. In the mood of post-war hope and euphoria, Israel had just offered the Arabs a return to the Armistice Lines, with minor changes only for Jordan, in exchange for peace. The Arabs spurned that offer and announced instead a policy of "no negotiations, no recognition, no peace."

At one point, Ambassador Dobrynin asked whether UNSC 242 meant only minor changes in the Armistice Lines for Jordan. On being told that so far as the U.S. was concerned, that was the present position of the Israeli government, but that, if the Arabs persisted in their rejectionist policy, our view of the territorial questions might well change. "Resolution 242 permitted very different outcomes, and security considerations were serious." Dobrynin said that on that basis, the Soviet Union could agree to that interpretation and accepted it. The next day, he telephoned to report that he would have to withdraw his approval. Evidently, his government had decided to have its cake and eat it too, if it could. The Soviet Union repeated the Arab line about UNSC 242 until it expired, and the Russian government has not yet disclosed its hand.

UNSC 242, then, leaves the issue of territorial settlement to the agreement of the parties. It was, however, negotiated with a boundary between Israel and Jordan in the foreground. The U.S. has remained firmly opposed to the creation of a third Palestinian state on the territory of the Palestine Mandate. An independent Jordan or a Jordan linked in an economic union with Israel is desirable from the point of view of everybody's security and prosperity, and a predominantly Jewish Israel is one of the fundamental goals of Israeli policy. There is, therefore, no objective reason why these conflicting claims cannot be reconciled in the negotiations now being held. On the other hand, the risk that Arab negotiators might be murdered if they sign such agreements is a factor they can never ignore.

UNSC 242 was distilled with great pain from the agony of the prolonged Arab war against Jewish settlement in Palestine. It is a fair compromise and offers a fair foundation for a just and lasting peace.

Vernon Turner

I have been waiting for twenty-five years to talk about this subject, and the time has finally come.

I was asked to relate my recollection of the debate over the wording of the resolution and my understanding of the intent of the drafters, so I shall try to do that. I should say that as a student at university, I rather liked a German historian, Ranke, who felt that it was possible to present history "wie es eigentlich gewesen ist," as it actually was. And I am going to try to do that, although I have no illusions about the complexity of the challenge I face.

What became known as Resolution 242 was the product of many minds and many pens. All members of the Security Council, with the possible exception of Nationalist China, had a hand in it. In the General Assembly, a variety of member states submitted proposals and tried to influence events. The Non-Aligned and the Latin American countries were particularly active.

Ultimately, it fell to Lord Caradon of Great Britain to devise the winning formulation which carried the day in the Security Council on November 22, 1967.

The key elements in UNSC 242 had been in play since the Six Day War. We all knew what they were: withdrawal of forces, termination of belligerency, freedom of transit through international waterways, a solution to the refugee problem, a peaceful settlement, and the appointment of a special representative of the Secretary-General to help bring that about.

The challenge at the UN was how to deploy some or all of these elements in a resolution which would attract maximum support, preferably in the Security Council, and obtain, at the same time, at least the acquiescence of the parties directly concerned. Room for maneuver was confined by certain realities: on the one hand, the strengthened position of Israel as a consequence of the war and her determination not to return to the *status quo ante*, and on the other hand, the continuing adherence of the Arab states to a policy of no recognition and no direct negotiation with Israel.

The several resolutions adopted by the Security Council in the first ten days after the outbreak of war concentrated on the need for a cease-fire and the cessation of all military activities. One resolution condemned any and all violations of the cease-fire. Another was of a humanitarian nature. None of these resolutions mentioned withdrawal. And as Justice Arthur Goldberg said in something I read this morning, this was not an accident. All of the Council members realized that the question of withdrawal must be addressed, but some members, including Canada, were convinced that this could not be done without regard to the situation which had existed before the war broke out.

In the immediate pre-war period, we had been particularly troubled—by "we," I mean Canada—by incidents between Israel and Syria in the demilitarized zone, and then dismayed by the closure of the Straits of Tiran to Israeli shipping. We did not want to help recreate a situation in which such events could occur again.

In the light of such events, Canada and Denmark requested an urgent Security Council meeting in late May and sought support for an appeal for restraint to all parties concerned. Our anxiety at the time had been sharply heightened by the sudden withdrawal of UNEF from Sinai and Gaza and by the Secretary-General's assessment that the situation in the Near East was "more menacing than at any time since the fall of 1956."

The Canadian-Danish initiative of late May was resisted by the Soviet Union and others, only to be overtaken by the war itself. Now, belatedly, the Council was fully engaged. Initially, Canada worked to strengthen the Secretary-General's hand in ensuring compliance with the cease-fire resolutions. When that seemed assured, we placed increasing emphasis on the desirability of sending a special representative of the Secretary-General to the Middle East to help in reducing tensions and restoring peaceful conditions.

On June 14, we circulated informally a draft resolution to that effect to other members of the Council and to the parties. Our text mentioned neither withdrawal nor termination of belligerency nor the other key elements. Clearly, it was not meant to be the last word, but we believed it was the most useful thing which the Council could do quickly. An intermediary with a broad, non-contentious mandate could at least, we thought, start to deal with the consequences of the recent conflict.

Perhaps our approach was too pragmatic. In any event, debate shifted to an emergency session of the General Assembly, where many member states were adamant that any resolution must explicitly state the requirement for withdrawal of Israeli forces. Canada's own position on this was clear. Speaking to the General Assembly on June 23, Secretary of State for External Affairs Paul Martin said "If peace and security are to be assured, the withdrawal of Israeli forces... must be related to the other basic issues involved."

This notion of linkage was not palatable to many member states in June. At the emergency session, the Soviet Union and a group of non-aligned states endeavored, separately, to obtain approval of one-sided condemnatory resolutions which would have contributed nothing to the achievement of withdrawal or the solution of any other outstanding problem. Fortunately, they failed.

Concurrently, a group of Latin American states submitted their own draft resolution which did link between withdrawal and other issues, and in particular, ending the state of belligerency. This draft also failed. Interestingly, the Latin American resolution requested Israel "to withdraw all its forces from all the territories occupied by it as a result of the recent conflict." This was a stronger, more precise formulation than later appeared in UNSC 242.

Neither the Non-Aligned draft nor the Latin American draft said anything specific about boundaries, although the Latin American text did call on the Security Council, rather inelegantly, to work to guarantee the territorial inviolability of the states of the region.

Against the background of these developments, the Latin Americans in July consulted among themselves on revisions to their failed draft while the Soviets looked for a way out. It was, after all, the Soviet Union which had demanded the emergency session of the General Assembly and had a strong vested interest in a substantive outcome. With its prestige at stake, the Soviet Union showed signs of being prepared to adopt a more flexible, more balanced approach than had been evident since before the Six Day War.

The Soviets, taking a revised, partly-agreed Latin American draft of July 18 as a basis, floated two variations behind the scenes, and these variations marked a turning point in behind-the-scenes negotiations. The second of these variations went to the heart of the matter, and in terms of equity, was arguably better than anything the Latin Americans had produced. The second Soviet formulation struck a balance between "withdrawal by the parties to the conflict of their forces from territories occupied by them," and "acknowledgment by all member states of the UN in the area that each enjoys the right to maintain an independent national state of its own and to live in peace and security and renunciation of all claims and acts inconsistent therewith."

The Soviet variations never surfaced formally at the General Assembly because of Arab objections, but they did show that the concept of linkage between withdrawal and other issues had been accepted by the Soviet Union.

In pursuing its variations, the Soviet Union consulted the United States and appears to have achieved a large measure of agreement. Whatever was agreed between the two superpowers was increasingly referred to as the Dobrynin-Goldberg variations. This had a nice ring to it, but the deadlock remained. The emergency session adjourned without adopting any substantive resolution on withdrawal and belligerency.

After the traditional August hiatus, diplomatic activity shifted back to the Security Council. In September, the permanent members searched for a formula that the parties could live with, but positions seemed to have hardened. A major argument turned on whether withdrawal should be to positions occupied by Israel before June 5, a formula advocated by the Non-Aligned in the General Assembly. This was known to be anathema to Israel, which, it was increasingly believed, was unlikely to respect any call for withdrawal unless, in fact, it was to recognized boundaries.

As nothing emerged from the permanent members of the Council, the non-permanents, the other ten members, including Canada, became active in mid-October. In this group, the concept of linkage between withdrawal and other issues was accepted, but differences arose once again over how to strike a balance between them. There was something called a Six-Power Text submitted by Ethiopia, Nigeria, Mali, Brazil, India and Argentina, which was countered by a Danish draft co-sponsored by Canada. These two documents pointed up once again the gap in positions, and indeed, the gap seemed wider than ever, with the result that Canada and Denmark then attempted to bridge this gap by producing a composite text on October 31, combining the Six-Power version and the Danish-Canadian version.

This was our last best effort. It was not good enough, however, for reasons that can only be understood by comparing competing texts. The Six-Power draft stated that "Israel's armed forces should withdraw from all the territories occupied as a result of the recent conflict," whereas the Canadian-Danish composite text stated, "The sovereign existence, territorial integrity and political independence of every state in the area should be respected and acknowledged, and none of the states in the area should maintain forces on the territory of another state against its will or persist in refusing to withdraw them."

Canada and Denmark realized that their formulation on withdrawal of October 31 was soft by comparison with the Six-Power Text, or, indeed, by comparison with the Latin American resolution which Canada had voted for in the General Assembly in July. We considered, however, that the kind of linkage that we now proposed was necessary to produce concrete results.

It was one thing to support in the Assembly a resolution which could be no more than a statement of opinion and whose political weight would be diminished by a large number of negative votes and abstentions. It was something quite different to strive for a Security Council resolution which must not only be devoid of a veto, but ideally should be adopted unanimously if its principles were to be heeded by the parties to the conflict.

By early November, the ten non-permanent members had reached an impasse and returned the conundrum to the permanent members. In doing so, the non-permanents reported that they had achieved a consensus on three points. First, the appointment of a special representative. Second, that the special representative should have a specific mandate. And third, that the Security Council was acting under Chapter 6 of the Charter. In other words, it was establishing principles, making recommendations, it was not purporting to engage in enforcement action.

At this stage, the United States moved to the fore once again and produced its own variation of the Canadian-Danish composite text. The United States draft provided for withdrawal, but only as one of several elements required for the achievement of a just and lasting peace; and the draft included the term, I believe for the first time, "secure and recognized boundaries."

While the non-permanents and then the United States had been promoting various texts, Lord Caradon of Great Britain had been keeping in touch with Council members as well as with the parties in the Middle East, and he had been biding his time. He had declined to comment in detail on any of the different texts in play. Once it was clear to him that the non-permanents had exhausted their possibilities and that the United States was running into difficulties, Lord Caradon made what proved to be the crucial move. On November 12, he produced informally the text of a possible resolution, and on November 14, in the light of consultations, a slightly altered version. His goal in these consultations—I hope I do him justice—as I believe he saw it was to meet Israel as much as possible on security and the Arabs as much as possible on withdrawal.

On November 16, Lord Caradon tabled a polished draft resolution in the Security Council and steadfastly resisted all suggestions for change. Lord Caradon's final text included the famous, ambiguous call for "withdrawal of Israeli armed forces from territories occupied in the recent conflict," and balanced this with the right of all states in the area to live in peace within "secure and recognized boundaries."

The Arabs did not like the lack of precision in relation to withdrawal and said so. Nor did they like the word "recognized" in relation to boundaries. They tried to persuade Lord Caradon to amend his draft resolution both before and after it was tabled in the Council. Caradon held his ground. Kuznetsov of the Soviet Union asked Caradon to specify "all" before the word "territories" and to drop the word "recognized." When Caradon refused, the Soviet Union tabled its own draft resolution, but it was not a viable alternative to the UK text and could only be seen as a public relations gambit designed to show where the Soviet Union stood before she was obliged to take a position on Lord Caradon's proposal.

On November 22, 1967, immediately before the vote, certain members of the Security Council placed upon the resolution before them interpretations designed to make the imprecise precise. Lord Caradon obviously did not wish to be drawn into a battle of conflicting interpretations lest it upset the prospects for success. The resolution, he asserted, must be viewed as a balanced whole. What the Security

Council had before it, he added, was "the resolution, the whole resolution, and nothing but the resolution."

With that declaration sounding in the Council's ears, members voted and adopted the resolution unanimously. In the view of Ambassador George Ignatieff, speaking for Canada, the resolution entailed an "equitable balance of obligations" and represented a "fair, balanced and non-prejudicial basis" for the dispatch to the Middle East of a special representative of the Secretary-General. That was true, but Canada's faith in the efficacy of personal diplomacy by a UN intermediary proved misplaced. The special representative grappled with the issues for several years without result.

What proved to be of enduring value and what we remember today is the resolution's framework for a just and lasting peace in the Middle East. UNSC 242 has provided the context for all subsequent efforts to achieve a peaceful settlement. It was reaffirmed in UNSC 338 following the Yom Kippur War and recalled as the basis for a settlement in the Camp David Accords. Whatever else it does, UNSC 242 still represents the silver lining in the clouds which gather from time to time over the peace process.

I like to think that all those minds and pens in 1967 did not labor in vain.

PART II

LEGAL INTERPRETATIONS OF UNSC 242

Meir Rosenne

It is a real privilege to be here this morning and to have the opportunity to meet many "survivors" of the peace negotiations—Kilometer 101, Camp David, and the rest. As the Canadian Ambassador noted a moment ago, I have been waiting some eighteen years to have the opportunity to come here and share some of my perceptions of UNSC 242 as a basis for the peace settlement in the Middle East.

The negotiations that took place after the adoption of this resolution and the legislative history of this document leave no doubt that it is *only a framework*. As the Secretary-General of the UN, Boutros Boutros-Ghali, had the opportunity to reiterate on March 19, 1992, it was adopted under Chapter 6, not Chapter 7, of the Charter of the UN.

Furthermore, the resolution is *a list of general principles* which can become operative only after detailed and specific measures have been agreed upon. As one distinguished diplomat has stated, "the parties must put flesh on these bare bones."

It is equally clear that the detailed elements of these principles have to be negotiated by and between the parties. This is illustrated by the fact that there is a special representative to assist the parties to reach agreement. On a more substantive level, there is a reference to "secure and recognized boundaries," which means that the previous boundaries were neither secure nor recognized. The boundaries are obviously one of the main issues that need to be fleshed out in the negotiations.

In my humble opinion, UNSC 338 does not add anything as to the binding effect of UNSC 242.

Moreover, the language of UNSC 242 clearly refers specifically to states: the reference is to "the states concerned." It does not even name the states concerned, which means that it applies not only to the states that are Israel's immediate neighbors who were involved in the actual fighting, but also to the other states in the area that are still in a state of war with Israel.

Does UNSC 242 apply to the Palestinian Arabs? I think not. The letter of invitation to the Madrid conference, for example, contains a reference to UNSC 242 and the Palestinians, but it is clear from the wording of this invitation that it does not apply to the interim self-government arrangements. There are two reasons for this: (a) the resolution itself applies only to states; (b) the resolution does not deal with autonomy or any transitional period (that is provided for in a later document, the Camp David Accords).

There is another point that needs clarification: the preamble's reference to the "inadmissibility of acquisition of territory by force." This resolution, in all its parts, forms the basis for the Camp David Accords. How is it that, during those long negotiations at Camp David, Israel agreed to a document which refers to a document that incorporates this principle in the preamble?

First of all, the resolution deals with the acquisition of territory, *not* military occupation. There is nothing in any source of international law—customary law, conventions, etc.— that makes military occupation illegal.

If I correctly interpret the intentions of the resolution's drafters, the inadmissibility of acquisition of territory by force means that mere occupation does not entitle one to acquire territory. It does not give you legal title to sovereignty.

Without entering into legalistic details, I might note that there is a debate in international law about the legality of the acquisition of territory as a result of a war which was itself an act of self-defense. Opinions are divided, but one thing is extremely clear: there is nothing in the Charter of the UN or in any facet of international law that makes the mere occupation of captured territory until a peace treaty can be signed illegal.

During the debate over UNSC 242 in the Security Council, India, Mali, and Nigeria proposed a text that stated "Occupation or acquisition of territory by military conquest is inadmissible under the Charter of the UN." This proposed text was never adopted. This paragraph on withdrawal refers basically to three independent principles: (a) the inadmissibility of the acquisition of territory by war; (b) the need for a just and lasting peace; (c) the need for security.

There is ample evidence as to the fact that the withdrawal was not from *all* territories. Joseph Sisco, then U.S. assistant secretary of state, on July 17, 1967, stated that "That resolution did not say 'withdrawal to the pre-June 5th lines'."

Similarly, Michael Steward, British secretary of state for foreign and commonwealth affairs, answering a question in Parliament in 1969 about whether the resolution required that Israelis should withdraw from all territories taken in the 1967 war, said, "No, sir. That's not the phrase used in the resolution. The resolution speaks of secure and recognized boundaries. Those words must be read concurrently with the statement on withdrawal." On another occasion he mentioned that "The omission of the word 'all' before the word 'territories' is deliberate."

George Brown, who was the British foreign secretary in 1967, stated in 1970 that "The proposal said 'Israel will withdraw from territories that were occupied', not 'from the territories,' which means that Israel will not withdraw from all the territories." In short, the boundaries have yet to be negotiated.

There is a debate as to the discrepancy between the French text and the English text. Since this matter has been raised many times, it is should be noted that, in international law, if there is any difficulty in interpreting the language of texts, the original text is used as the reference point. Since the resolution was a British proposal, it is the English text that prevails. Incidentally, of the members in the Security Council at that time, English was used by ten members, French by three, Russian by one, and Spanish by one.

A question has arisen over whether the acceptance of the Camp David Accords constitutes a precedent for future negotiations between Israel and the Arab states, especially since Israel and Egypt did conclude a peace treaty based on the accords.

Indeed, the Camp David Accords refer to an understanding between Egypt and Israel which could be interpreted as some kind of precedent. Referring to the two states, it says "They, therefore, agree that this framework, as appropriate, is intended by them to constitute a basis for peace."

So does it serve as a precedent? The answer seems obvious. The peace treaty between Israel and Egypt was the result of negotiations between sovereign states, and any agreement that was accepted and signed by both parties is binding, with or without UNSC 242. It was a bilateral negotiation with the indispensable assistance of the U.S., without which there would not be peace today between Israel and Egypt—even after the signing of the Camp David Accords on September 17, it took six months to negotiate the peace treaty between Israel and Egypt, with the active participation of the U.S.

This treaty is not a precedent for the delineation of the borders. Indeed, the borders between Israel and each of the Arab countries still remain to be negotiated, with the possible exception of one border, the border with Lebanon. It was, by the way, on Arab insistence that the Armistice Agreements of 1949 contain a specific provision stating that these are armistice lines and not final boundaries, which means that the boundaries have still to be negotiated.

This is further confirmed by Syria's outright rejection of UNSC 242 after its adoption on November 22, 1967. Syria stated, at the highest level of government, that this resolution is totally unacceptable because it does not imply an obligation for Israel to withdraw from all the Syrian territory occupied in the 1967 war. So boundaries still need to be negotiated.

So too with the determination of claims of belligerency, recognition, and secure boundaries.

Additionally, UNSC 242 refers not merely to right of passage, but to freedom of navigation, a much broader right. This matter was satisfactorily taken care of in the agreement with Egypt. But there are other riparian states with which this problem has to be negotiated. Jordan and Saudi Arabia, both coastal states of the Gulf, still need to guarantee freedom of navigation through the Straits of Tiran and the Gulf of Aqaba.

Although UNSC 242 refers to the "just settlement of the refugee problem," the Palestinian issue was not addressed in 1967. But the legislative history of UNSC 242 (illuminated in a very interesting article written by the late Ambassador Arthur Goldberg) shows that there was a proposal to refer explicitly to "Arab refugees," but this was not even submitted to a vote let alone adopted.

The reason for the rejection was that we, for our part, raised the problem of Jewish refugees who had been expelled from Arab countries. There were about 650,000 Arabs that left the territories then under Israeli control, but 800,000 Jews had been expelled from Arab countries, and the question of their compensation is still open. It should be made clear that in this resolution, the reference to refugees does not only apply to Arab refugees.

There are other problems that are being discussed today in the negotiations in Washington and other capitals of the world—the environment, regional cooperation, water, etc. These issues were not mentioned in UNSC 242 because the basic problem at that time was to reach agreement on a document that would prevent a further outburst of war or hostilities.

In conclusion, UNSC 242 requires that the parties negotiate in good faith in order to reach agreement on these guidelines: withdrawal of Israeli forces to secure and recognized boundaries established by agreement; termination of the state of belligerency, including any economic boycott which is certainly illegal under international law; and the recognition by all parties of each other's independence and statehood.

As for UNSC 338, adopted by the Security Council after the 1973 Yom Kippur War and the disengagement agreements signed by Israel and Syria, its main significance is that it is the first time that Syria accepted UNSC 242.

UNSC 242 is still very much alive. If you examine the history of the UN, this is certainly the only document that has helped so much in reaching at least a first peace treaty between an Arab state and Israel.

Nabil Elaraby

I am delighted to be here today to address the legal interpretation of UNSC 242. I was present at the creation. I was in the Security Council chamber when the resolution was adopted in 1967. I do not recall that my colleagues in the Egyptian delegation or I were overwhelmed with joy when it was adopted—relief maybe, but definitely not joy. The reason is not that we considered the resolution inadequate or defective, but rather that we were surprised that it took the international community several months to pronounce itself on such an important matter as the June 1967 war.

What remains relevant today is that it was adopted unanimously, and it was both confirmed and strengthened, as many have already stated today, by UNSC 338 in 1973. The resolution was applied only once, in different stages, which respect to the Egyptian front, and I will come to all this in due course.

I would like at this juncture to maintain proper perspective. The Security Council had one objective in mind when it adopted UNSC 242—the establishment of a just and lasting peace in the Middle East, an objective confirmed by all fifteen Security Council members and by the concerned parties in the region. I do hope that before long, comprehensive peace will prevail and UNSC 242 will be studied by historians as a valuable, constructive document without any ambiguities.

In the course of its twenty-five year life-span, UNSC 242 has been both praised and vilified. Yet detractors and admirers alike agree that UNSC 242 has dominated the diplomatic scene as the only acceptable basis for establishing a viable, just, and comprehensive peace in the Middle East. UNSC 242 is a multidimensional resolution with political, legal, territorial, and human dimensions. I do not intend to enter into several of the issues. I will confine myself to the legal interpretation of what is called the territorial dimension, which actually has been addressed by many before me. In doing so, I will not touch upon or address the question of the political rights of the Palestinians, although it is a very important matter. I stand by what I said a few moments ago, that in 1967 the thrust of the Arab position was territorial.

The question of the rights of Palestinians was confined to a just settlement of the refugee problem, by which I mean that the Palestinian refugees have the right, in accordance with UN General Assembly Resolution 194 of 1948, to choose between repatriation or compensation and which has been introduced every year and co-sponsored by the U.S., including this year. This resolution is therefore considered the basic term of reference for the Palestinian refugees in accordance with the international community. However, I am not going to address the issue of Palestinian rights, which only developed later and which is now the heart and soul of the Palestinian problem. Instead, I will address only the territorial dimension.

In the course of presentations today, we have listened to attempts to portray UNSC 242 as an ambiguous resolution which could be interpreted as endorsing the acquisition of territory by war. I do not subscribe to such views. My presentation has one main purpose, namely to defend UNSC 242 and to demonstrate that the Security Council was acting within the basic norms of international law and the purposes and principles of the UN Charter.

It should be emphasized that notwithstanding the intentions and understandings of certain concerned parties, UNSC 242 is a Security Council resolution. It is important to remember that the resolution was not a private deal between certain actors in the international community. This is a major flaw, if I may submit, in what has been said today. Regardless of who was the founding father, who were the parents, and who was the midwife, it should be remembered that the resolution is a UN document. It had to be in accordance with the Charter of the UN and the general principles of international law. We have heard from the U.S. undersecretary of state at that time what

President Johnson thought. Yes, he said all these statements. No one denies this. But he could have gone with Mr. Kosygin and brought the parties and wrote a treaty somewhere regardless of the UN and put whatever they wanted to put there. It would have been valid. Having gone to the UN, however, we cannot come today and say "This is the interpretation of Mr. So-and-so or President So-and-so or Prime Minister So-and-so." We have to base our interpretation on the law of nations. The recollection of the participants are therefore of limited importance, and the resolution has to be interpreted on the basis of the UN Charter. This is a very important point which I would like to make at the very beginning.

The jurisprudence of the United Nations has been consistent and quite clear. It was pertinently stated by the late Secretary-General Dag Hammarskjold in a 1957 report (Doc. A/3512): "The United Nations cannot condone a change of the *status juris* resulting from military action contrary to the provisions of the charter. The organization must therefore maintain that the *status juris* existing prior to such military action be re-established by a withdrawal of troops and by the relinquishing or nullification of rights asserted in territories covered by the military action and depending upon it." This has been the position of the UN and will remain the position of the UN, and by that I mean the position of the international community as a whole.

Let me start at the beginning. Following the unanimous adoption of the resolution, Mr. Abba Eban, then foreign minister of Israel stated that: "I am communicating to my government for its consideration nothing except the original English text of the tract as presented by the original sponsor on such-and-such a date."

This is quite unprecedented. All official and working languages are authoritative and hence have equal effect. Mr. Eban, of course, as I am sure everyone here knows, is a renowned linguist, but he chose to single out one text, the English text. He did not refer to any other, despite being able to speak fluent French. The French text, of course, says, "des territoires" which is always referred to as "the territoires." I did not count who was present of the fifteen, but I take what my colleague Meir Rosenne said as valid. I would remind him, however, that the president was a native French-speaker from Mali, and did not speak one single word of English, and he read every resolution in French. Nevertheless, this being a very minor point, I will not make anything of it.

The absence of the definite article "the" in the English text has been stretched, distorted, and presented to the world as if the UN Security Council endorses and condones acquisition of territories through the use of force. Through a well-orchestrated public relations campaign, a myth has been created around the absence of the definite article "T-H-E." And this point really has been blown out of proportion. What weight does the absence of this definite article hold?

First, I will make some general legal observations. The proponents of the definite article argument, and many are present in this room, allege that the omission of the definite article overturns the edifice of legitimacy which is solidly anchored in jurisprudence and philosophy of the UN Charter. The principle of the inadmissibility of the acquisition of territory by force emanates from the 1928 Kellogg-Briand Pact; its corollary, the non-recognition of such acquisition of territory, emanates from the 1932 Stimson Doctrine. Both the Stimson Doctrine and the Kellogg-Briand Pact were the work of American secretaries of state.

Article 51 and Article 2, Paragraph 4, of the UN Charter refer to these two basic doctrines while prohibiting the use of force in international relations altogether. Contemporary international law makes it clear that the territory of a state shall not be occupied without its consent.

In 1967, Israel alleged that its military attack was defensive in nature. Today, we heard in the very lucid presentation by Professor Rostow that the "closing" of the

Straits of Tiran was the first shot fired. Well, I wonder how that can be?

The government of Egypt did not break any agreements in 1967. And I stand to be corrected, if anyone will show me or refer me to any document saying that Egypt has signed on such a matter. Egypt had accepted in 1956-57 the presence of a UN force by the border in Sinai.

With respect to this defensive nature, I refer everyone to what has been written by the leaders of Israel—who planned the attack, who fired the first shot, what was done at that time. I will not enter into that as it belongs to history and is well-known. Nothing in the UN Charter impairs the right of self-defense if an armed attack occurs, but, in 1967, the Arabs were not the first to attack. The Charter recognizes the right of self-defense only "until the Security Council has taken measures necessary to maintain international peace and security."

The second point I would like to make here is that when we address a legal interpretation of UNSC 242, the standard term of reference is the 1969 Vienna Convention on the Law of Treaties. Paragraph 3 of Article 31 in the Vienna Convention makes it very clear that subsequent practice is a very important element in application and interpretation of any agreement. Article 32 stipulates that recourse may be taken in terms of supplementary means of interpretation in order to confirm the meaning when it becomes clear that an interpretation "leads to a result which is manifestly absurd or unreasonable."

A third point which is important, and again, distinguished speakers today have said that UNSC 242 was adopted under Chapter 6 of the UN Charter. Yes, I agree—Chapter 6, Article 37, Paragraph 2, which requires the Security Council to recommend such terms of settlement as it may consider appropriate, is probably the reference. Others have claimed that the draft resolution did not make any reference to a specific article or chapter of the UN Charter and that all Security Council resolutions that deal with armed conflicts which threatens international peace and security are binding. At the very beginning of the United Nations that was done, and then, due to many reasons which I will not get in to, this practice was dropped. But I agree, UNSC 242 was adopted under Chapter 6, and here I will say to those who allege that the Security Council, in adopting UNSC 242, condoned that non-withdrawal from all the territories, that a recommendation cannot be binding on anyone. I do not think you can have your cake and eat it. If you agree that UNSC 242 is under Chapter 6, then you accept that the matter has been put to the parties; this is a point which I will just leave now and come back to in a moment.

The resolution was adopted as a balanced package, as first advanced by the 1971 Jarring *aide-memoire*. There exists some confusion over the resolution's binding nature and whether the resolution is in fact self-implemented. The resolution was definitely not self-implemented because Paragraph 3 of the resolution provides for the appointment of a special representative to proceed to the area and promote an agreement in order to achieve a peaceful settlement in accordance with the provisions of UNSC 242. The Security Council itself has given ample indication that it felt the parties required assistance to implement UNSC 242, and the obligation to implement UNSC 242 has remained valid and binding on the parties.

In 1973, the Security Council decided that the parties should immediately implement the provisions of UNSC 242. Now my point is that maybe the question of whether it was binding or not in 1967 could be debated. I will leave this point moot. The parties have entered into contractual agreements (such as the Egyptian-Israeli Peace Treaty and the Syrian-Israeli Disengagement Agreement) which reaffirmed their acceptance of UNSC 242. In any event, all the parties accepted the invitation to the Madrid conference in November 1991 which contained an explicit reference to UNSC 242.

It is important to recall that the Security Council resolution was preceded by events. In order to understand it, one has to look at the events that preceded the language of the resolution, and attempts to implement it. I will discuss three of them.

With respect to events that preceded it, which might be called *travaux-preparatoires*, many speakers have referred already to two draft resolutions—one by the Latin American group and one by the Non-Aligned group. The U.S.—and here again I stand to be corrected—and Canada, and all the other Western countries voted for the Latin American group text.

What did the Latin American text say? The Latin American text, Document L-523 of June 30, 1967, urgently requests "Israel to withdraw all its forces from all the territories occupied as a result of the recent conflict." The Non-Aligned text contains a similar provision. Between the two drafts, every single member of the UN did vote for withdrawal from all the territories. The so-called Dobrynin-Goldberg variation merely couched the language in different ways, but it affirmed the principle of the inadmissibility of the acquisition of territory through the use of force and it called for immediate withdrawal from the territories occupied after June 4, 1967. These were the three documents that were really relevant here as there were some documents on one side and some on the other.

But the two General Assembly resolutions, the Latin American and the Non-Aligned, were never adopted. Egypt and the other Arab countries voted against the Latin American text. Why? Because it drew a link between withdrawal and an end of belligerency. So, the international community did not say whether withdrawal has to be from all the territories or not. The question at that time was, "are there any conditions for withdrawal?" And I say "yes, there were conditions." It took some time for the Arab states to accept, but there are conditions—to end the belligerency and to live in peace. And that was the basis of UNSC 242.

Now I come to the textual content of the resolution. The rationale and philosophical approach of UNSC 242 is to present the parties with a package of corresponding rights and obligations which conform to the UN Charter. The resolution's various provisions merit close examination.

With respect to UNSC 242's reference to "secure and recognized boundaries," I would like to stress that the withdrawal clause is clear. It does not mean "new" secure and recognized borders, but secure and recognized "existing" borders. The second part in the resolution refers to "termination of the state of belligerency," and that is addressed to every single party—both to Israel and the Arab countries. They can all live within secure and recognized boundaries. It has nothing to do with withdrawal; if it did, the resolution would have said so.

The call for Israeli withdrawal is directly linked to the preamble which refers to the inadmissibility of the occupation of territory by war and reminds all UN member states of their commitment to act in accordance with Article 2 of the Charter. It makes it incumbent to observe the law of the Charter scrupulously.

Now, Ambassador Rosenne proffered a very interesting argument—that there is a big difference between acquisition and occupation. Well, that is simply a question of title. I am happy that he said that because I would not get into the question of whether acquisition or occupation will lead to title or not. He spared me this point.

But the other matter that we need to discuss is that occupation on the basis of what? I mean, you cannot use force to break into your neighbor's home and say, "No, no, no, I'm occupying it. I don't have title." You cannot do that in interstate conduct.

Now, I have to get into the third part, which is the subsequent practice. Let's look at how the Security Council resolution has been implemented. The resolution made it clear that the special representative who was charged with implementing the provisions of the resolution was supposed to proceed to the area to promote agreement. The special representative did go to the area several times between 1968 and 1971, and then he came to the same conclusion as those dealing with the first Palestine war in 1948—start with the Egyptian front. That is the conclusion of Ambassador Gunnar Jarring, the special representative in 1971.

He submitted an *aide-memoire* to permanent representatives to the UN of both Egypt and Israel on February 8, 1971. It was the first serious substantive document presented to the parties to implement UNSC 242. The document had the same concept of corresponding rights and obligations of the resolution itself. He asked Israel to give a commitment to withdraw its forces from occupied United Arab Republic (as Egypt was then called) territory to the former international boundary between Egypt and the British mandate of Palestine—i.e. from all occupied Egyptian territory. So the balance of rights and obligations became clear when you entered the implementation phase. What was the answer to the first real attempt to implement UNSC 242? Egypt accepted it, but Israel rejected it. Had there been a positive reply from the two sides, maybe those who died in 1973 would not have lost their lives in vain.

The second attempt to implement UNSC 242, not counting the disengagement agreements to which Dr. Rosenne referred as they were limited in character, was Camp David, and the subsequent peace treaty of March 26, 1979. In that treaty, Israel was committed to withdraw all its armed forces behind the international boundary between Egypt and mandated Palestine—the same formula, more or less, of Jarring. I would request those who referred to the Armistice Demarcation Lines to look at the Armistice Agreement of 1949. The Egyptian-Israeli Armistice Agreement, signed on February 24, 1949, sets the same international boundary as the Armistice Demarcation Line apart from Gaza. The Armistice Demarcation Agreement refers to the international boundary, if my memory does not fail me, between ten and twelve times.

So the question of boundaries was there. And nowhere in UNSC 242 was there any attempt to say "new boundaries".

I will repeat, maybe for the third time, secure and recognized boundaries are not in the withdrawal clause at all. There is no call from the Security Council for the parties to "Change your boundaries." Nowhere. That is the question of the subsequent practice.

Now, in conclusion, all Security Council resolutions should meet the test of lawfulness by being compatible with the purpose and principles of the UN Charter as well as the general principles of international law. The Council would be exceeding its competence if it were to decide to change boundaries or act contrary to the law of the Charter. Obviously, the Council has not done so. The territories occupied in 1967 should be de-occupied. Any other assertion would be a travesty of legal norms as well as, to quote the Vienna Convention, "manifestly absurd and unreasonable."

The parties no doubt are entitled to modify and rectify their boundaries. All states in every part of the world have that sovereign right. The United States has adjusted its border with Mexico, and could do the same with Canada. My country could do it with Libya, and actually did do so in 1926. UNSC 242 did not add or detract from this general practice of inter-state conduct.

I submit that there is cogent and irrefutable evidence in fact and in law that the myth created on the flimsy and fallacious argument of the so-called definite article, should really be dismissed by now. What weight to the absence of the definite article "the"? The answer is none whatsoever. UNSC 242 calls for the restoration of the territorial *status quo ante*. In the words of former presidential candidate, Ross Perot, "I rest my case."

PART III

THE ORIGINS AND RELEVANCE OF UNSC RESOLUTION 242

Adnan Abu Odeh

When my friend Dr. Robert Satloff invited me to talk to this symposium, he was fair in his request that I explore the relevance of UNSC 242 to the peace process twenty-five years after it was passed rather than talk about its legal aspects, a field which I do not specialize in.

With all my respect and friendship for Dr. Satloff, I say very frankly and truthfully that I hesitated in giving him a final answer when he called me. The reason for my hesitation was because I knew I would be talking at a symposium organized by an institute known to be very close to the Israeli lobby.

After long reflection and consideration of the matter, I felt that what I would say might contribute positively and indirectly to the peace process underway. In this sense, it might be an expansion of the efforts of the Arab and Israeli negotiators to reach a peace agreement based on UNSC Resolutions 242 and 338. I thought that, irrespective of the opinions of either the Arab or Israeli sides regarding the relevance of negotiations to UNSC 242, and whether they are taking place on its basis or for the purpose of its implementation, the resolution does constitute the common ground on which they meet. Although several months elapsed before each negotiating side submitted the written proposals to the other negotiating side, their arrival at this state means that they have begun to transform from adversaries to professional fellows bent on handling a common problem in order to reach a settlement that is accepted by the two parties and fulfills both their interests.

Out of all this, I came to the conclusion that progress has already been made, thanks primarily to UNSC 242. Thus, permit me to score at this early stage a point in favor of the resolution. But before I proceed to the subject of discussion, may I thank Mrs. Barbi Weinberg for her words in introducing me. Yet, inspired by the occasion, I do not find it irrelevant to expand a little bit on this matter and introduce myself to you.

I am from a Palestinian town called Nablus. For those who have not visited it, Nablus is a beautiful town situated in a wide valley stretching to the slopes of two mountains facing each other and looking down upon it like loving parents. I was born there in 1933. I grew up in it and learned in its schools. I lived in a house now classified as absentee's property, built by my father after the earthquake of 1927, which destroyed the big family house situated in what is called, in today's press language, the *Casbah*. I walked in the alleys of the *Casbah* and in the streets of the town. I played in its yards and climbed the north mountain where our house is scores of times with friends from the same quarter in springtime to pick wild narcissus and red anemone. I used to return with my share of them before sunset to my house, where my mother received me with a loving, thankful smile, taking the flowers from my hand and putting them in a vase on a table in the corner of the living room.

Nablus, like any other ancient town, is rich in its traditions, which are practiced collectively at every turn in a person's life. There are rituals starting with a child's birth, his entering school and completing study of the Koran, his graduation from high school and university, his marriage and his death. Nablus, like any other town, has its traditions during religious holidays, particularly during the months of Shabban and Ramadan. All these traditions are accompanied by songs, religious and non-religious anthems, and Koran readings. Nablus also has its seasonal traditions, including Persian Norouz and Thursday picnics during spring. Even bathing at the public Turkish bath in Nablus has a tradition.

Except for death, these are all happy occasions which together constitute a collective consciousness for the people of Nablus. It is still so, particularly for those who left or were forced to leave. These traditions are, for the people of Nablus, a pleasant topic they like to talk about wherever they meet, whether in Amman or Riyadh, Washington or Montreal, Sydney or Frankfurt, or in any other place. Together they form the national unwritten covenant among them, and recollecting them during their meetings breathes ever-renewed life in this covenant.

Practicing these traditions within the framework of the family in foreign countries gives the people of Nablus their distinct identity, of which they are proud. The news on television screens which shows women and children clashing with soldiers of the occupation army, particularly in the past five years, makes us feel that the repressive reaction of the Israeli soldiers to our compatriots' rejection of the occupation are but blows of axes on our roots meant to make us bleed to death. This town of mine whose tradition I practice or remember and teach to my children in order to emphasize our identity, the occupation authority has given another name as an expression of their desire to wrest it from us. I wonder if this authority is aware that by doing so, it has provided the people of Nablus with a new bond of attachment to their hometown.

Please pardon me if I have digressed or if I seem to introduce emotion into a subject that requires reasoning. My aim is not to thrill, but to emphasize that the idea of perpetuating *faits accomplis* in occupied Palestine will not bring peace and security to the disputants and that UNSC 242 is the only sail remaining on the ship that has been sailing in a sea of fear and uncertainty for more than four decades, carrying on board both Palestinians and Israelis.

Having all this in mind, I accepted the invitation of my friend Dr. Satloff, hoping to row with those who are rowing in an effort to bring the ship to the shore of peace and security.

My talk is going to be divided into two major interrelated themes: first, the political implications of UNSC 242; and second, time as an actor on the stage of dispute in the Middle East.

Now, let me address the first theme. Throughout the last quarter of a century, UNSC 242 has become the litany of the political literature of the Middle East. The fact that it constitutes a major term of reference for the ongoing negotiations indicates that it is viable and tenacious. Its viability and tenacity, in my opinion, are due to the fact that it is both balanced and susceptible to balanced development. The reasons why it came out as a balanced resolution are as follows:

First, in view of the fact that the Soviet Union's prestige was at stake among the Arabs after their military defeat in 1967 and the fact that the Vietnam War was at its climax, the U.S. and the USSR seemed serious in their endeavors to avoid direct confrontation, particularly in the Middle East, which is of strategic importance to the world because of its vast oil resources and its proximity to Europe and the former Soviet Union.

Second, it was passed following the third war between the same disputing parties in an area whose states were split into two camps. One camp was a friend or an ally of the Western bloc, and the other was a friend or an ally of the Eastern bloc.

Third, it was the fruit of consultation among representatives of the Cold War blocs and leaders of the conflicting states.

Fourth, it was based on the principles of the UN Charter.

The balance that marks UNSC 242 is reflected in both the spirit and text of the resolution. The spirit of the resolution, as summarized in its preamble, is that peace and territorial conquest are incompatible. The inadmissibility of the acquisition of territory by force is its guiding principle. No linguistic ambiguities override this guiding principle.

The resolution, by basing peace on the twin requirements of security and withdrawal, refutes and negates the notion of security through territorial gain. It makes the two incompatible and contradictory. Any interpretation of UNSC 242 to the contrary is semantical acrobatics. UNSC 242 required the simultaneity of withdrawal on one hand and recognition and security on the other. One cannot be made a prior condition for the other. Furthermore, UNSC 242 requires a just solution of the problem of refugees, as defined by UN General Assembly Resolution 194 of 1948.

As I said, UNSC 242 is not only balanced but, in its spirit, susceptible to balanced development. Since its passage a quarter century ago, the resolution has expanded to incorporate two new elements without affecting the principles on which it is based. These two elements are:

First, Israel's acceptance of the Arab and international demand that Palestinians participate in the ongoing negotiations after the PLO had accepted UNSC 242, despite the fact that when UNSC 242 was passed, it was understood to refer to the belligerent states only.

Second, Arab acceptance of the Israeli demand that they normalize relations with her after a peace agreement is reached despite the fact that normalization is not provided for by UNSC 242. Paragraph (a), article 2, simply affirms the necessity "for guaranteeing freedom of navigation through international waterways in the area." What is meant here is freedom of navigation in the Tiran Straits and in the Aqaba Gulf. Had the resolution required or visualized more than that, it would have provided for such a requirement or visualization without confining itself to freedom of navigation, which is considered to be secondary in comparison with the policy of normalization.

Palestinian participation and working to achieve the goal of normalization are a balanced development of the resolution compatible with its spirit which reflects the aspiration for the establishment of durable, just, and comprehensive peace in the area.

If it is customary for the victor to seek to acquire booty from its triumphant war, Israel has acquired precious booty in its victory in the war of 1967. The booty was implied in UNSC 242, which not only called on Israel to withdraw from the territories it occupied, but went beyond that to affirm respect for and acknowledgment of the sovereignty, territorial integrity, and political independence of every state in the area and their right to live in peace with secure and recognized boundaries free from threats or acts of war. Acceptance of this text by the Arabs means they have accepted the notion of the booty to the victorious.

To realize the importance of Arab acceptance of UNSC 242, we should recall the Arab attitude toward Israel from 1948 until November 1967. All of us are aware that the Arab attitude was based on non-recognition of Israel and seeking ultimately to dismantle it; in other words, they rejected the existence of Israel as a state in the Arab region. All of us are also aware that this Arab attitude constituted the basis on which Israel was acting nationally in its armament policy and internationally in its diplomacy and media policy.

This Arab attitude did not change abruptly after the June 1967 war. The three Khartoum 'Nos' are known to you. In fact, the Arabs sustained this attitude until UNSC 242 was passed in November 1967, though their public position continued well beyond that.

The Israeli media policy, in turn, continued to cite the former Arab attitude until the signing of the Camp David Accords, despite the acceptance by Jordan and Egypt of UNSC 242 in 1967 and Syrian acceptance of UNSC 338 in 1973. With the acceptance by Jordan and Egypt of UNSC 242, a drastic turn took place, and an important new trend in the history of the region started, a trend toward establishing peace that accommodated the Jewish state as one of the Middle East states. That is a decisive trend, thanks to UNSC 242.

Yet the most ironic thing about this profound change is that both the Arab states and Israel deliberately endeavored to submerge it, each for its own reasons. Israel, for its part, found in the emergence of the Palestinian resistance, which was accompanied by violence, a good reason for effacing this important gain of acceptance. Israel was hoping to achieve other gains in the form of additional concessions by the Arab side, forgetting that the booty of the battle is usually won by the victor after the dust of the battle settles. And Israel had already taken its booty.

Israel's demand today for more Arab concessions, particularly in terms of territory, strike Arab sentiment as attempts to humiliate them and usurp their rights. Persisting on such demands will definitely not be conducive to the success of the peace process that is currently underway.

I realize intellectually and emotionally what it means for Israel to win Arab acceptance. Israel, through UNSC 242, has achieved the most important strategic goal that has obsessed her and governed her policies since she came into being—the goal of being accepted in the Arab region and not to be viewed as an alien body. Such a view would mean negation of real Israeli security. Talking about Israeli security in this context would mean, in the final analysis, shaking the belief in the basis of the Zionist movement. In my opinion, this could be the main reason why the Israeli government and the Israeli media deliberately avoided talking about this big gain.

The Arabs, for their part, chose not to talk about important implications of UNSC 242, namely, their readiness to accept Israel. They chose instead to focus on the withdrawal of Israel from the occupied Arab territories. They did that because they realized the magnitude of the concession they presented to Israel as a war booty, which they later obtained as a result of defeating them. It was difficult for the Arab governments to face their peoples with that. Therefore, both Israel and the Arabs, each for their own reasons, participated without coordination in effacing the most important development in the history of the Arab-Israeli relationship. If the Israeli handling of the question of acceptance did not help in speeding up the building of a peace camp in Israel, Arab handling did not help them in gaining more international understanding of their positive attitude toward peace.

However, there is a very important issue which UNSC 242 does not address and which the Arab-Israeli dialogue and the Arab-Palestinian dialogue have not developed any reasonable concept about.

Until the June war of 1967, the parties to the conflict were identified as Arab states on one side and Israel on the other side. The Palestinian independent actor was invisible because it was merged into the Arab bloc. UNSC 242 reflected this reality. The Palestinian component in the conflict was referred to in UNSC 242 in an indirect manner. Operative item 2 states that the Security Council "affirms further the necessity... for achieving a just settlement of the refugee problem." Yet the Israeli occupation of the West Bank and Gaza Strip, the continuity of that occupation and the Palestinian resistance to it have contributed to the emergence of the independent Palestinian actor that has imposed itself on the scene of the conflict and has gradually won a world-wide recognition, including in Israel itself. The Israeli-Palestinian track in the ongoing bilateral negotiations is an evidence to that.

The formulators of UNSC 242 had not preconceived these developments—the long duration of the occupation and the emergence of the Palestinian actor. Their concept was based on the fact that the Middle East conflict was between Israel and the Arab states that rejected the recognition of the State of Israel. They felt that if peace was to be reached in the Middle East after three wars between the parties, the Arab states had to recognize Israel, which, for its part, had to withdraw from the Arab territories it occupied as a result of war. The resolution in general was a reflection of this concept. The Arab states understood that, by accepting UNSC 242, they implicitly recognized Israel, that they would reach a state of non-belligerency with Israel, that they would regain the territories they lost in the war, and that peace, as a result, would be established.

The formula of "population, land, and identity" was not in the minds of any of the three parties, Israel, the Arab governments, or the Security Council. As I have mentioned earlier, the long duration of the Israeli occupation and the susceptibility of UNSC 242 to develop in a balanced manner have contributed to major developments: first, the Arab states have accepted the notion of real, or full peace, or normalization as the ultimate objective of a peaceful settlement; second, the Israeli position has developed to the point where it accepts the Palestinians as their own interlocutor. With this second development, it has become imperative that the "population, land, and identity" formula be addressed seriously and as soon as possible, simply because of the ramification of the existence of millions of Palestinians in Israel and in the abutting Arab states.

Israel was the first party to integrate this issue in its peace strategy. All of us are aware of how the Jewishness of the state of Israel and its democracy are adversely affected by the Palestinian territories it occupies. And no wonder about that, since Israel is an occupying power encountering all the time Palestinian rejection and resistance.

On the other hand, neither the concerned Arab governments nor the PLO has addressed this issue since their efforts are being focused on Israeli withdrawal and the establishment of a Palestinian state. The terms of reference of the ongoing direct negotiations, to my understanding, do not address this issue in clear terms. Besides, the format of the negotiations is designed on the compartmentalization model. There are both bilateral and multilateral negotiations. The bilateral negotiations are broken down into a Palestinian-Israeli track, a Jordanian-Israeli track, a Syrian-Israeli track, and a Lebanese-Israeli track, while the multilateral negotiations consist of five working groups, one each for arms control, refugees, environment, economic development, and water.

The compartmentalization approach could be very useful if the parties are aware of and agree upon the general framework of the endgame. This cannot be realized unless the "population, land, and identity" formula is worked out. The various parties involved in the negotiations should, in my opinion, be alerted to and aware of this dimension. A conceptual framework for the end game should be reached so that the parties—especially the Israelis, the Palestinians, and the Jordanians—can use one compass in their joint journey toward peaceful agreements. The earlier they do that, the faster the pace of negotiations will be.

I proceed now to talk about the second theme, the theme of time. I am not going to talk about time from the perspective of a chronicler of events—that is something common and well known. Rather, I shall talk about changes that took place over a period of twenty-five years, and the new outlook of parties to the dispute, people and governments.

Some changes have had an adverse impact on the peace process, while others have had positive ones. I shall refer to three adverse changes. First, the radical political right in Israel gradually expanded in the Israeli political spectrum and reached the summit in the 1980s. In light of the Israeli elections last June, however, it seems to have lost some ground. The Arab right is in a state of growth and expansion, and its effect on the public is increasing. Both rights are now posing to see the failure of the peace process, hoping to derive from its failure a new momentum.

Second, the long suffering of the Palestinian people under the occupation, which they reject by all the means available to them.

Third, the rise of the Israeli settlers on the occupied territories as a militant constituency against the land-for-peace formula.

On the other hand, there are also positive changes.

First, the left in Israel still constitutes one of the most important bulwarks of the Israeli peace camp. In comparison, the Arab left, which was once considered radical, has become more moderate, adding a new force to the Arab peace camp, particularly after the end of the Cold War.

Second, Arab political thinking has started to shift, albeit slowly, from the concept that international conflicts are solved by litigation to the familiar concept that they are solved through balancing the interests of the antagonists. There is no doubt that this is a major, far-reaching development and a qualitative addition to the quest for peace. The concept of litigation, which has dominated the Arab mind since the start of the Arab-Israeli dispute, was responsible, in my opinion, for allowing the Arabs to miss valuable opportunities for peace during the past six decades. The ingredients of this concept lie in the roots of the Arab pastoral value system.

Third, the elapse of twenty-five years since the passage of UNSC 242 has contributed toward extracting Israel gradually from the complex of security based on acceptance. Sadat's visit to Jerusalem and the Camp David agreements in particular contributed to this development, which manifested itself in the Israeli rhetoric the 1980s.

Fourth, the continuation of Israeli occupation of Palestinian land for twenty-five years has pushed the question of the relationship between the area of Israel and the democracy and Jewishness of the state to the forefront of Israeli political thinking.

Fifth, UNSC 242 says nothing about the necessity of developing a peace culture between the Arabs and Israel. But the elapse of twenty-five years since the adoption of the resolution and the continuous direct and indirect dialogue that revolved around its implementation have contributed, together with the new international trend toward peace, to an increased awareness of international interdependence following the end of the Cold War. All have contributed to gradual acceptance of this important dimension in the desired peace structure—a culture of peace.

Sixth, the Camp David agreement and the Arab reconciliation with Egypt after the Amman Arab summit in 1987 have familiarized the concept of peace and the acceptance of Israel.

Seventh, the official and popular Arab attitude prior to the 1967 war was that the region would never enjoy peace and stability until Israel was destroyed. Now the official and popular Arab attitude is that the region will never enjoy peace and stability until the Palestinian people exercise their right to self-determination on their national soil. Let us think carefully about this development, to appreciate the qualitative change that took place twenty-five years after the resolution was passed.

Finally, and most importantly, the Arab-Israel dispute has changed from a dispute between two nationalities into a territorial dispute over dividing the land of Palestine between the Jewish people and the Palestinian people. That is a great development.

Nevertheless, I would warn of two things:

First, Israel should not imagine that the mere elapse of time will produce more opportunities for them to achieve more gains. I warn against such a conclusion because the Arabs have reached the breaking point, and the breaking point with people is not the same as with metals. When a metal reaches the breaking point, it merely breaks, but people become temporarily silent, storing grudges and differences, and prepare for another round.

Second, the question of Jerusalem. I would like to emphasize that none of the Arab negotiators can sign a peace treaty with Israel without a just and acceptable settlement reached on the question of the city of Jerusalem. I hope the Israelis will not deceive themselves by embracing the logic of the precedent, relying on the fact that Egypt reached a peace agreement with Israel without a mutually acceptable solution to Jerusalem. The fact is that the Egyptians believe on both the official and popular levels that the Egyptian-Israeli peace treaty is only a prelude to comprehensive peace, not only in the sense that a comprehensive peace will include all parties that will sign peace agreements, but also in the sense that a settlement will solve all problems, particularly the problem of the status of Jerusalem.

To elaborate more, I would say if we suppose that the negotiating Arab parties reached a settlement now for all outstanding problems except Jerusalem, that would raise again for the Egyptians the question of Jerusalem, because they will discover that the peace which they sought is not complete. I am sure all of us are aware of the Egyptian religious disposition, especially in this period of time.

Therefore, I believe that the bridge to genuine, durable peace based on UNSC 242 should be laid on the following foundations:

One, Israeli withdrawal from the occupied Arab territories, including Arab Jerusalem;

Two, the Palestinian people exercising their right of self-determination on their national soil;

Three, official Arab recognition of the state of Israel;

Four, an acceptable just settlement for the problem of Jerusalem;

Five, meeting the internal and external security requirements of Israel and the Arab states;

Six, openness of the parties to the concept of cultural and regional economic cooperation;

Seven, settlement of the water issue on the basis of water rights of the states concerned and providing fair shares for them;

Eight, a balanced practical formula for the "population, land, and identity" issues that engulf Israel, Palestine, and Jordan.

UNSC 242 is the only prescription for Arab-Israeli peace to enjoy the unanimous support of the international community as well as the parties to the conflict. For this reason, it was identified as the framework for the peace process, and it is for this reason that it must not be interpreted away. The Israeli view, expressed during the sixth round of talks in Washington by Itamar Rabinovitch, chief Israeli negotiator with Syria, that UNSC 242 is only "background music" for the peace process, undermines the only agreed approach to the Arab-Israeli peace process.

UNSC 242 is balanced and susceptible to balanced development. It has survived all the political fluctuations and military confrontations in the area during the last twenty-five years.

UNSC 242, intended to bring about comprehensive regional peace, necessarily means that it applies to all fronts, all parties, and all phases of the conflict resolution process. Its application to any of the bilateral relations does not negate or weaken its applicability to others. Partial or separate agreements, even if based on UNSC 242, threaten the integrity of the peace process by casting doubt on the comprehensive applicability of the resolution.

The passage of Resolution 338 in 1973 affirms that UNSC 242 is to be implemented, not bargained away. Negotiations should center on how it is to be implemented, not on which parts to implement. UNSC 242 reflects the prevailing international consensus today. Its implementation is not only the fulfillment of a twenty-five year-old resolution, but also of the current commitment of the international community.

In the invitation letter I received, I was asked to examine the relevance of UNSC 242 after twenty-five years of its endorsement. In the analysis I have made and which I have presented to you this morning, yes, I firmly believe that UNSC 242 remains extremely relevant. It has not only weathered the test of time, but it has survived all political vicissitudes of the region. Many times I have heard His Majesty King Hussein express his satisfaction and pride for having contributed to its drafting. Having examined UNSC 242 the way I did today, I now understand why.

PART IV

UNSC 242 AND ARAB-ISRAELI PEACEMAKING

Dennis B. Ross

It is quite remarkable to think that we are here commemorating the twenty-fifth anniversary of UNSC 242. If nothing else, that certainly highlights that this is a Security Council resolution that has durability. And there are probably a variety of reasons why it has had durability. It has offered a political explanation for many of the parties in the area for when they talk about peace, it has offered a reference point that they could all agree on when they have dealt with the question of Middle East peace. Even though UNSC 242 does not make any direct reference to the political dimension of the Palestinian question, it has been a reference point for Palestinians as well, and I think that further highlights the centrality of UNSC 242 to the process.

One other indication of its centrality is that every important peacemaking effort in the region has had UNSC 242 at its core—the Camp David process and the Egyptian-Israeli Peace Treaty were both underpinned by UNSC 242. The terms of reference that we put together to launch the process that began in Madrid also had UNSC 242 as a critical element or core principle embodied within it. When a resolution of this sort lasts this long as a reference point for everybody, and continues to underpin the approach to peace, there has got to be something right with it.

Now I know that you had long discussions on UNSC 242 and its meaning, and the roots of it, and the origins of it. And I am not really interested in getting into that discussion or replaying that discussion. In fact, what I would like to do is make one observation about UNSC 242 which may, in fact, bear some relevance to the discussion that you had this morning, and use that as a springboard to talk about the peacemaking process and where we are today.

That observation is that there is a kind of inherent paradox with UNSC 242. A friend and colleague of mine, Aaron Miller, has referred to it as the "242 paradox." By that he means that, on the one hand, there is a kind of clarity with regard to UNSC 242 as a reference point, as a core principle. On the other hand, there is an ambiguity with regard to its terms and its meaning.

On the way to Madrid, I can tell you that there were a lot of hard issues that we had to tackle, a lot of issues that were addressed more than once, a lot of hard nuts that had to be cracked. One of these that was raised repeatedly by a number of parties was whether the U.S. could remove the ambiguity in UNSC 242. Indeed, some claimed that we needed to adopt a position that in looking at UNSC 242 and its constituent parts and the relationship of peace, and withdrawal, and security, removed the ambiguity and provided a precise definition. Every single time this was raised, we said no. We said that removing the ambiguity would mean prejudging the negotiations, and that is not what our role is about. Instead, Secretary Baker went out several times in several places in the Middle East, and he said there are different interpretations to UNSC 242. The parties are going to bring those different interpretations to the table. They are going to go ahead, and they are going to remove the ambiguity; to provide the definition, they are going to provide the meaning. And that is really the essence, over time, of what this process that we put together is all about. It is not for the United States to provide that; in the end, the parties are going to do that.

Where are we in this process that we've succeeded in putting together? Anybody who knows me knows that whenever I pose questions, I never take the easy way in answering them. This is an old device that I have found useful, it allows me to cover a lot of ground. I usually like to create some context in which to evaluate questions. So, to gain some context and perspective on where we are in the process today, one needs to think about where we have come from.

Madrid was launched thirteen months ago. If I take you back fourteen months, let me describe the process of trying to promote peace, and where we were. Fourteen months ago, there was still a taboo that basically said Arabs and Israelis cannot meet or talk directly. This fundamental taboo has been broken; that threshold has been crossed. And the fact the negotiations have been going on for over a year might indicate to some that the we are not making a lot of progress; on the other hand, this says something about the durability, as well, of peacemaking. And to put that in perspective again, let us bear in mind what it is we have—bilateral direct negotiations as well as multilateral negotiations.

Take a country like Syria. Syria has always been the focal point of Arab nationalism and of pan-Arabism, and it has always seen itself as the leader of the confrontation states. Syria has been engaging in bilateral negotiations with Israel over the course of the last thirteen months. The significance of that is hard, I think, to exaggerate. Psychologically, it has an impact in the area; psychologically, it sends a message to everybody in the area about how much the area is changing.

Fourteen months ago, the hardest nut that we had to crack was how to sort out the question of Palestinian representation in negotiations. This issue basically brought Camp David to a halt and blocked every effort to promote peace after Camp David, and this is an issue that, again, we have overcome. For the last thirteen months, you have also seen negotiations between Israelis and Palestinians.

Fourteen months ago, if I had said that we would be able to broaden the Arab orbit that was dealing with Israel and have multilateral negotiations, and there would be thirteen Arab states engaged in both bilateral and multilateral talks with Israel, and Syria would be one of them, I would bet that most of the people in this room would have said, "No way, you simply won't get that."

Again, it is a measure of the psychological change that has taken place, and also the very first point I made. There has been an impact in the area that has resulted just from this process. Something has happened in the past fourteen months. Something happened when we were able to get to Madrid. What happened was that we did not just cross a threshold, we basically replaced diplomacy through denial with the diplomacy of engagement.

A diplomacy of engagement does not guarantee either success or instant gratification, nor does it mean you are necessarily going to get where you want to go, but if you do not have diplomacy of engagement, you are guaranteed to get nowhere. So at least we have a first important step.

What has happened in the negotiations themselves over the course of these last thirteen months? Here, again, I would say there has been an evolution, and I think you have to look at phases or stages that any set of negotiations, especially among adversaries, are going to go through. The first phase of this negotiation was characterized by the fact that such a meeting was an event. Events are occasions for posturing; they are not occasions for negotiating. Events are occasions for parties talking *at* each other, not *to* each other. That should not have come as any major surprise since the talks involved parties that had not previously negotiated or met.

We were dealing with parties that in the past had their views, their beliefs, their fears, their suspicions, their objectives always interpreted by others to the parties they were now dealing with.

Now they had an opportunity to express these views, these fears, and these suspicions directly. To think that we would not go through a phase that would involve venting, a release, explaining oneself, explaining one's sense of grievance was not realistic. To think that we would go through a phase where the parties would not, in fact, talk *at* as opposed to *to* each other was also not particularly realistic. So we went through that phase.

Prior to the Israeli elections in June 1992, I began to see some signs that maybe the parties would begin to talk to each other and not just at each other. There is no doubt that with the advent of a new Israeli government the ability to "talk to," as opposed to "at," became much more pronounced. We began to see much more of an actual engagement between the parties, and the engagement produced long, searching discussions on a variety of issues. Indeed, these discussions have covered almost every conceivable issue, and have been characterized by great detail. These kinds of discussions, I think, are a prelude to what is required for negotiations to make headway.

There is a certain sociology in negotiations, especially between adversaries. You have to go from "talking at" to "talking to," to acquiring what I call the problem-solving mentality. Just because you are engaged does not mean you have acquired the "problem-solving" mentality. Look at the negotiations that we and the Soviets had, whether it was in arms control or in dealing with regional conflicts. We went through each of these phases, and it took an awfully long time to get to the point where there was a problem-solving mentality.

In these negotiations I can tell you that in some, but not all, of the bilaterals, I have begun to see signs of a problem-solving mentality. I have also seen it in some, but not all, of the multilaterals. There is an effort conceptually to create a problem-solving approach, and that is good news because it shows there is a continuing evolution and it means that things have moved from where they began.

Now again, this is not a guarantee of success or of any instant breakthroughs. But it is an indication that things are moving in the right direction even if the progress is not as quick as some might like.

As we look ahead, I would note that in my mind, especially at this particular juncture, there are two kinds of environmental factors that are going to influence this process, given where it is right now. The first factor is what I call realities on the ground. These negotiations do not take place in a vacuum. They do not take place in isolation. You cannot somehow feel these negotiations can be put off to the side and things can happen on the ground and not affect them. They are going to affect them.

There are certainly some who will use violence to try to subvert the process because they do not believe in the process to begin with. We saw in this last round that there was violence in Lebanon, and it clearly had an impact on this negotiating round. For the Israelis, you are not only talking about Lebanon, but about the territories. The Israeli impulse to lighten the burden or the character of control or occupation is obviously going to be shaped by whether or not there is violence in the territories. The more active Hamas is, the more difficult it becomes to take certain kinds of steps. But not easing the character of occupation will not make it easier for Palestinian negotiators. Taking steps that might ease the occupation could be important to Palestinians when they look at the kinds of things that they might do that might make the negotiations more productive. So obviously both Israelis and Palestinians are going to be affected by the climate and by the environment.

If there is a hiatus in the negotiations, those who are determined to subvert the process and are willing to use violence to that end will take advantage of that hiatus. And that obviously is something that is dangerous from the standpoint of trying to insulate this process and promote it and develop it.

But before we despair, I want to relay a discussion I had with one of the Arab delegates in this last round. He had come to see me, and we were talking about the violence in Lebanon. I was giving him my impression of some of the consequences of this and how it might affect negotiations. And he said to me, "Well, of course, you are right. And, you know, Hezbollah has been active; Israel has retaliated. But let me remind you of something. The negotiations have gone on, and you in particular should not underestimate the fact that negotiations have gone on."

It is an interesting reminder. It is a reminder that if you never entered a process, it is pretty easy to step away from it. But once you have crossed a threshold and gone into it, you develop and acquire a stake in it. And it is not so easy to step away from it. And that is important as we think about how to deal with those who may try to subvert the process.

It is also important in terms of dealing with what I consider to be the second environmental factor that affects the process, given where it is right now, that we are in a period of transition. And because we are in a period of transition, that creates a variety of different kinds of temptations. It creates a temptation on the part of the parties to do a lot of different things because they are now suddenly dealing with unknowns and uncertainty. They do not deal real well with unknowns and uncertainties, and therefore it is not all that surprising that that is the case.

They will be tempted to probe, to revisit issues that maybe were taken care of before, and to seek a different kind of American role. There will be a variety of temptations, none of which ought to be feared, none of which should be seen as necessarily a major problem from the standpoint of this process. All of them are quite natural.

These temptations have to be managed. Now, from my particular standpoint, and maybe it is a peculiar one, I think it is very important to do as much as we can between now and January 19 to pin things down as well as we can. We should try, in other words, to create as much of a road map as possible so that the new administration that is coming in will inherit more than it would be inheriting today. But not simply so that they can inherit more. The real value in creating the road map is to create enough specificity and understandings on the issues to be discussed, the sequence in which to discuss them, enough concreteness in terms of how to proceed, so that the parties during this period of inevitable familiarization will have a sense of direction to carry them through, to sustain the kind of momentum that is necessary, and also a clear-cut framework with which to proceed so that the impulse to test and probe will be somewhat limited.

The familiarization process is a given. Just like probing is going to be a given, so is the familiarization process. It has to happen, and it is not a question of learning what has been discussed. That is easy to convey. The familiarization process relates much more fundamentally to all the parties getting to know who the new administration is going to be, what the attitudes are going to be, how it is going to proceed, and whether or not the parties can trust the people they are going to be dealing with.

You do not create that overnight. We did not create it overnight. It cannot be done overnight. And it is critical. The whole notion of trust is critical because you are dealing with parties that from their standpoint are either making life-and-death decisions in this process, or they are making the most important political decisions they have ever undertaken. But when the U.S. is as critical a player in this process as we are and you are asking these kinds of parties to undertake these kinds of decisions, they are not going to make those decisions until and unless they are satisfied that they can count on the people that they are dealing with.

Trust is not a function of agreement. Trust is a function of making commitments and following through on the commitments. I have said many times, the measure of a commitment is not that you follow through on the commitment when it is easy to do so; the measure is that you follow through when it is hard to do so. You are talking about parties that are going to need to see that if you give your word on something, you deliver on it. They need to be sure that you won't violate some of your own principles that you have established. So, if you are going to succeed, you are going to have to develop that trust.

And one of the reasons it is so important is that you are dealing with parties that see themselves taking fundamental decisions as central and as critical as any they could take, and if they go out on a limb, they want to know the U.S. is not going to chop it off. Instead, if they go out on a limb, they want to know we are going to insulate them against the pressures that are inevitable, we are going to reassure them against the risks that they see themselves running. They want to know that we can be counted on when they have to do things that are difficult for them. And that is a major part of the American role; it is not the only part of the American role.

Another part of the American role is to be what I call a lubricant of this process. People use lots of different terms: "catalyst," "facilitator." You know, I get bored with the old terms, so I invented a new one—"lubricant." Why do I say "lubricant"? What does it mean? "Lubricant" means that when you run into problems, there is someone there to ease the way. "Lubricant" means when you hit roadblocks, you come up with ways to get around the roadblocks by working with the parties.

Sometimes you are there to reassure the various parties against what they are hearing directly from the other side. Oftentimes, and this is part of this process that has been repeated on any number of occasions—I cannot tell you how many times—one party will say something to the other, will mean one thing, and what is heard is entirely different. And so you are going in there to disabuse them of certain incorrect interpretations. Sometimes you are going to reaffirm that what they are hearing is the right thing and they can build on it. Sometimes we may be called on to make suggestions or ideas where the parties themselves decide that they might be able to do something but they cannot be the ones to initiate a particular idea and it is easier if we do it.

There are all sorts of things that we can do and will have to do if this process is going to succeed. I can tell you from experience that what I am suggesting is not easy. In fact, I can tell you it is damn hard at times. But it is worth it because you have to think about what the alternative to this process is going to be. We have built a set of expectations. The parties do have a stake in this process. But if it does not pay off, if it does not yield results, then what we have done is create an environment where those who claim that negotiations cannot work have an argument to make, and we can see that there are those in the area who are determined to subvert the process. We know there are extremist elements committed to that. We can look at what Hezbollah is doing in Lebanon and what Hamas is doing in the territories. They are much more likely to represent the future if we do not succeed, so it is worth it to preempt that possibility because if they succeed and we do not, then we are going to see another war, only the next war will be fought with very different kinds of weapons than the last war or the preceding wars. So it is worth it to preempt that possibility.

And it is worth it also because there is a unique opportunity now that has not existed before. There is an opportunity to build a genuine peace in this region. And I hope that when you have another meeting on UNSC 242, and I am not anticipating that you wait another twenty-five years, we will be able to say UNSC 242 was not just a reference point, but a benchmark to a pathway that produced peace. It produced a new day in the Middle East so that construction replaced destruction, so that reconciliation replaced estrangement, so that hope replaced hatred, and so that the Middle East, in fact, had a period of peace for its future and not a perpetuation of its past.

DOCUMENTS

SECTION A: SELECTED UN DOCUMENTS

Non-Aligned Draft Resolution	71
Latin American Draft Resolution	73
American Draft Resolution	75
India, Mali, and Nigeria Draft Resolution	77
Soviet Draft Resolution	79
UN Security Council Resolution 242	81
UN Security Council Resolution 338	83

SECTION B: SELECTED STATEMENTS BY U.S. OFFICIALS ON UNSC 242

Arthur Goldberg, November 15, 1967	85
William Rogers, December 9, 1969	87
Joseph P. Sisco, July 12, 1970	88
George Bush, December 5, 1972	89
John Scali, July 14, 1973	89
Alfred L. Atherton, Jr., April 5, 1978	93
Walter Mondale, July 2, 1978	95
Harold Saunders, January 29, 1979	95

Ronald Reagan, September 1, 1982	96
George P. Shultz, September 10, 1982; April 5, 1988; September 16, 1988	97
James Baker, May 17, 1991	99
George Bush, October 30, 1991	99
Bill Clinton, November-December, 1992; March 15, 1993	103
Edward Djerejian, March 8, 1993	105

SECTION C: SELECTED DOCUMENTS

The Camp David Accords	107
Treaty of Peace between Egypt and Israel	118
Invitation to the Madrid Conference	124

SECTION D: LEGAL INTERPRETATIONS

Arthur Goldberg	129
Eugene Rostow	136
Stephen Schwebel	144

SECTION A

SELECTED UN DOCUMENTS

Non-Aligned Draft Resolution

June 13, 1967

The General Assembly,

Having discussed the grave situation in the Middle East,

Noting that the armed forces of Israel occupy areas including territories belonging to Jordan, Syria, and the United Arab Republic,

1. *Calls upon* Israel to withdraw immediately all its forces to the positions they held prior to 5 June 1967;

2. *Requests* the Secretary-General to ensure compliance with the present resolution and to secure, with the assistance of the United Nations Truce Supervisory Organization established by the Security Council, strict observance by all parties of the General Armistice Agreements between Israel and the Arab countries;

3. *Requests further* the Secretary-General to designate a personal representative who will assist him in securing compliance with the present resolution and be in contact with the parties concerned;

4. *Calls upon* all States to render every assistance to the Secretary-General in the implementation of the present resolution in accordance with the Charter of the United Nations;

5. *Requests* the Secretary-General to report urgently to the General Assembly and to the Security Council on compliance with the terms of the present resolution;

6. *Requests* that the Security Council consider all aspects of the situation in the Middle East and seek peaceful ways and means for the solution of all problems—legal, political and humanitarian—through appropriate channels, guided by the principles of the Charter of the United Nations, in particular those contained in Articles 2 and 33.

Latin American Draft Resolution

June 13, 1967

The General Assembly,

Considering that all Member States have an inescapable obligation to preserve peace and, consequently, to avoid the use of force in the international sphere,

Considering further that the cease-fire ordered by the Security Council and accepted by the State of Israel and the States of Jordan, Syria, and the United Arab Republic is a first step towards the achievement of a just peace in the Middle East, a step which must be reinforced by other measures to be adopted by the Organization and complied with by the parties,

1. *Urgently requests*:

(a) Israel to withdraw all its forces from all the territories occupied by it as a result of the recent conflict;

(b) The parties in conflict to end the state of belligerency, to endeavor to establish conditions of coexistence based on good neighbourliness and to have recourse in all cases to the procedures for peaceful settlement indicated in the Charter of the United Nations;

2. *Reaffirms its conviction* that no stable international order can be based on the threat or use of force, and declares that the validity of the occupation or acquisition of territories brought about by such means should not be recognized;

3. *Requests* the Security Council to continue examining the situation in the Middle East with a sense of urgency, working directly with the parties and relying on the presence of the United Nations to:

(*a*) Carry out the provisions of operative paragraph 1 (a) above;

(*b*) Guarantee freedom of transit on the international waterways in the region;

(*c*) Achieve an appropriate and full solution of the problem of the refugees and guarantee the territorial inviolability and political independence of the State of the region, through measures including the establishment of demilitarized zones;

3. *Reaffirms*, as in earlier recommendations, the desirability of establishing an international régime for the city of Jerusalem, to be considered by the General Assembly at its twenty-second session.

American Draft Resolution

November 7, 1967

The Security Council,

Expressing its continuing concern with the grave situation in the Middle East,

Recalling its resolution 233 (1967) on the outbreak of fighting which called, as a first step, for an immediate cease-fire and for a cessation of all military activities in the area,

Recalling further General Assembly resolution 2256 (ES-V),

Emphasizing the urgency of reducing tensions and bringing about a just and lasting peace in which every State in the area can live in security,

Emphasizing further that all Member States in their acceptance of the Charter of the United Nations have undertaken a commitment to act in accordance with Article 2 of the Charter,

1. *Affirms* that the fulfillment of the above Charter principles requires the achievement of a state of just and lasting peace in the Middle East embracing withdrawal of armed forces from occupied territories, termination of claims or states of belligerence, and mutual recognition and

respect for the right of every state in the area to sovereign existence, territorial integrity, political independence, secure and recognized boundaries, and freedom from the threat or use of force;

2. *Affirms further* the necessity:

(a) For guaranteeing freedom of navigation through international waterways in the area;

(b) For achieving a just settlement of the refugee problem;

(c) For guaranteeing the territorial inviolability and political independence of every State in the area, through measures including the establishment of demilitarized zones;

(d) For achieving a limitation of the wasteful and destructive arms race in the area;

3. *Requests* the Secretary-General to designate a Special Representative to proceed to the Middle East to establish and maintain contacts with the States concerned with a view to assisting them in the working out of solutions in accordance with the purposes of this resolution and in creating a just and lasting peace in the area;

4. *Requests* the Secretary-General to report to the Security Council on the progress of the efforts of the Special Representative as soon as possible.

India, Mali, and Nigeria Draft Resolution

November 7, 1967

The Security Council,

Expressing its continuing concern with the grave situation in the Middle East,

Recalling its resolution 233 (1967) on the outbreak of fighting which called for, as a first step, for an immediate cease-fire and for a cessation of all military activities in the area,

Recalling further General Assembly resolution 2256 (ES-V),

Emphasizing the urgency of reducing tensions, restoring peace and bringing about normalcy in the area,

1. *Affirms* that a just and lasting peace in the Middle East must be achieved within the framework of the Charter of the United Nations and more particularly of the following principles:

    (i) Occupation or acquisition of territory by military conquest is inadmissible under the Charter of the United Nations and consequently Israel's armed forces should withdraw from all the territories occupied as a result of the recent conflict;

(ii) Likewise, every State has the right to live in peace and complete security free from threats or acts of war and consequently all States in the area should terminate the state or claim of belligerency and settle their international disputes by peaceful means;

(iii) Likewise, every State of the area has the right to be secure within its borders and it is obligatory on all Member States of the area to respect the sovereignty, territorial integrity and political independence of one another;

2. *Affirms further:*

(i) There should be a just settlement of the question of Palestine refugees;

(ii) There should be a guarantee of freedom of navigation in accordance with international law through international waterways in the area;

3. *Requests* the Secretary-General to dispatch a special representative to the area who would contact the States concerned in order to co-ordinate efforts to achieve the purposes of this resolution and to submit a report to the Council within thirty days.

Soviet Draft Resolution

November 20, 1967

The Security Council,

Expressing concern at the lack of progress towards a political settlement in the Middle East and at the increased tension in the area,

Noting that there have even been violations of the cease-fire called for by the Security Council in its resolutions 223 (1967) of 6 June, 234 (1967) of 7 June, 235 (1967) of 9 June, and 236 (1967) of 12 June 1967, a cease-fire which was regarded as a first step towards the achievement of a just peace in the area and which was to have been strengthened by other appropriate measures,

Recalling General Assembly resolutions 2252 (ES-V), 2253 (ES-V), 2254 (ES-V), and 2256 (ES-V),

Emphasizing the urgent necessity of restoring peace and establishing normal conditions in the Middle East,

1. *Declares* that peace and final solutions to this problem can be achieved within the framework of the Charter of the United Nations;

2. *Urges* that the following steps should be taken:

(a) The parties to the conflict should immediately withdraw their forces to the positions they held before 5 June 1967 in accordance with the principle that the seizure of territories as a result of war is inadmissible;

(b) All State Members of the United Nations in the area should immediately recognize that each of them has the right to exist as an independent national State and to live in peace and security, and should renounce all claims and desist from all its acts inconsistent with the foregoing;

3. *Deems it necessary* in this connexion [sic] to continue its consideration of the situation in the Middle East, collaborating directly with the parties concerned and making use of the presence of the United Nations, with a view to achieving an appropriate and just solution of all aspects of the problem on the basis of the following principles:

(a) The use or threat of force in relations between States is incompatible with the Charter of the United Nations;

(b) Every State must respect the political independence and territorial integrity of all other States in the area;

(c) There must be a just settlement of the question of the Palestine refugees;

(d) Innocent passage through international waterways in the area in accordance with international agreements;

4. *Considers* that, in harmony with the steps to be taken along the lines indicated above, all States in the area should put an end to the state of belligerency, take measures to limit the useless and destructive arms race, and discharge the obligations assumed by them under the Charter of the United Nations and international agreements.

UNSC RESOLUTION 242

Concerning Principles for a Just and Lasting Peace in the Middle East[1]

November 22, 1967

The Security Council,

Expressing its continuing concern with the grave situation in the Middle East,

Emphasizing the inadmissibility of the acquisition of territory by war and the need to work for a just and lasting peace in which every State in the area can live in security,

Emphasizing further that all Member States in their acceptance of the Charter of the United Nations have undertaken a commitment to act in accordance with Article 2 of the Charter,

1. *Affirms* that the fulfillment of Charter principles requires the establishment of a just and lasting peace in the

---

[1] UNSC 242 was adopted unanimously by all fifteen members of the Security Council: Argentina, Brazil, Bulgaria, Canada, China, Denmark, Ethiopia, France, India, Japan, Mali, Nigeria, USSR, United Kingdom, and the United States.

Middle East which should include the application of both the following principles:

(i) Withdrawal of Israeli armed forces from territories occupied in the recent conflict;

(ii) Termination of all claims or states of belligerency and respect for and acknowledgment of the sovereignty, territorial integrity and political independence of every State in the area and their right to live in peace within secure and recognized boundaries free from threats or acts of force;

2. *Affirms further* the necessity:

(a) For guaranteeing freedom of navigation through international waterways in the area;

(b) For achieving a just settlement of the refugee problem;

(c) For guaranteeing the territorial inviolability and political independence of every State in the area, through measures including the establishment of demilitarized zones;

3. *Requests* the Secretary-General to designate a Special Representative to proceed to the Middle East to establish and maintain contacts with the States concerned in order to promote agreement and assist efforts to achieve a peaceful and accepted settlement in accordance with the provisions and principles in this resolution;

4. *Requests* the Secretary-General to report to the Security Council on the progress of the efforts of the Special Representative as soon as possible.

UNSC RESOLUTION 338

Concerning The October War

October 22, 1973

The Security Council

1. *Calls upon* all parties to the present fighting to cease all firing and terminate all military activity immediately, no later than 12 hours after the moment of the adoption of this decision, in the positions they now occupy;

2. *Calls upon* the parties concerned to start immediately after the ceasefire the implementation of Security Council 242 (1967) in all of its parts;

3. *Decides* that, immediately and concurrently with the cease-fire, negotiations start between the parties concerned under appropriate auspices aimed at establishing a just and durable peace in the Middle East.

SECTION B

SELECTED STATEMENTS BY U.S. OFFICIALS ON UNSC 242

Arthur Goldberg, Permanent Representative to the UN
Statement to the UN Security Council, November 15, 1967

"... In my statement in the Council last Thursday I outlined the general considerations underlying this draft resolution. Let me now add certain specific comments on particular provisions in the hope of clarifying their meaning and intent in light of the comments made with respect to these clauses in the course of our debate.

"In paragraph 1, among the elements embraced in the concept of 'a state of just and lasting peace,' is 'withdrawal of armed forces from occupied territories.' Let me be quite clear about the meaning which we attach to this language. In the first place, it obviously refers and was always intended to refer to the armed forces of Israel; let me also state and make clear that this is completely on a par with the other essentials listed in the same statement: termination of claims or states of belligerence—which of course refers primarily to the Arab states. It also embraces a necessary ingredient for peace in the area: mutual termination by Israel and the Arab states of the state of war which unhappily still persists in the area and mutual recognition of, and respect for, the right of every state in the area to sovereign existence, territorial integrity, political independence, secure and recognized boundaries, and freedom from the threat or use of force.

"Mr. President, we thought that this concept was very clear in the resolution we offered; but since doubts have been expressed on this point we have clarified them, I think explicitly, today.

"Now, Mr. President, we believe that the language of paragraph 1 as stated in the resolution and as amplified by me here today is both intrinsically sound and carefully balanced in what it requires of the respective parties. And I should like to repeat them for emphasis.

"Israel must withdraw; the Arab states must renounce the state of belligerence and claim of belligerence which they have claimed for many years, and the states on both sides must terminate the present state of war and must mutually recognize each other's rights, which are set forth explicitly in article 2 of the charter...

"Now, I cannot emphasize too strongly that these principles are interdependent. There is nothing artificial about this interdependence; we did not manufacture it; it is in the nature of the situation and of the history of this conflict. To seek withdrawal without secure and recognized boundaries, for example, would be just as fruitless as to seek secure and recognized boundaries without withdrawal.

"Historically, there have never been any secure or recognized boundaries in the area. Neither the armistice lines of 1949 nor the cease-fire lines of 1967 have answered this description. The armistice agreements explicitly recognize the necessity to proceed to permanent peace, which necessarily entails the recognition of boundaries between the parties. Now, such boundaries have yet to be agreed upon—and agreement on this point is an absolute essential to a just and lasting peace, just as withdrawal is. Secure boundaries cannot be determined by unilateral action of any of the states; and they cannot be imposed from the outside. For history shows that imposed boundaries are not secure—that secure boundaries must be mutually worked out and recognized by the parties themselves, as part of the peacemaking process.

"I would add one further observation as to timing. Clearly, the timing of steps to be taken by the parties in fulfillment of the objectives set forth in the resolution we have tabled would need to be carefully worked out with the assistance of the special representative. It is not our conception that any one step or provision should be relegated to the end of the process.

"In short, Mr. President, our resolution reflects the conviction that progress toward peace can only be made if there is a careful and just balance of obligations among the parties. Such a balance must take account of the just aspirations of all without harming the vital interest of any. It must recognize and seek to relieve the legitimate grievances of all without creating new grievances for any. It must be a balance which all will have a strong interest in maintaining. Only thus can it provide the foundation for a durable peace..."

* * *

William Rogers, Secretary of State
Address to the Galaxy Conference, Washington, DC, December 9, 1969

"A lasting peace must be sustained by a sense of security on both sides. To this end, as envisaged in the Security Council resolution, there should be demilitarized zones and related security arrangements more reliable than those which existed in the area in the past. The parties themselves, with Ambassador Jarring's help, are in the best position to work out the nature and the details of such security arrangements. It is, after all, their interests which are at stake and their territory which is involved. They must live with the results.

"The Security Council resolution endorses the principle of the nonacquisition of territory by war and calls for withdrawal of Israeli armed forces from territories occupied in the 1967 war. We support this part of the resolution, including withdrawal, just as we do its other elements.

"The boundaries from which the 1967 war began were established in the 1949 armistice agreements and have defined the areas of national jurisdiction in the Middle

East for 20 years. Those boundaries were armistice lines, not final political borders. The rights, claims, and positions of the parties in an ultimate peaceful settlement were reserved by the armistice agreements.

"The Security Council resolution neither endorses nor precludes these armistice lines as the definitive political boundaries. However, it calls for withdrawal from occupied territories, the nonacquisition of territory by war, and the establishment of secure and recognized boundaries.

"We believe that while recognized political boundaries must be established, and agreed upon by the parties, any changes in the preexisting lines should be confined to insubstantial alterations required for mutual security. We do not support expansionism. We believe troops must be withdrawn as the resolution provides. We support Israel's security and the security of the Arab states as well. We are for a lasting peace that requires security for both..."

* * *

Joseph P. Sisco, Assistant Secretary of State for Near East and South Asian Affairs, interview on NBC-TV's "Meet the Press," July 12, 1970

"... Third, obviously withdrawal is a key element. Withdrawal from territories occupied during the June war is a key element of the UN Security Council Resolution of November 1967."

Mr. Spivak: "Withdrawal from all occupied territories?"

Mr. Sisco: "No, and this is what the argument is all about. The Security Council resolution calls for withdrawal of Israeli forces from territories occupied during 1967. I was engaged in the negotiations for months of that resolution. That resolution did not say 'total withdrawal.' That resolution said that the parties must negotiate to achieve agreement on the so called final secure and recognized borders. In other words, the question of the final borders, Mr. Spivak, is a matter of negotiations between the parties."

* * *

George Bush, U.S. Representative to the UN,
Statement to the UN General Assembly, December 5, 1972

"The heart of this resolution is that a just and lasting peace in the Middle East should include the applications of two—not one, but two—principles: withdrawal of Israeli armed forces from territories occupied in the 1967 conflict; and 'termination of all claims or states of belligerency and respect for and acknowledgment of the sovereignty, territorial integrity and political independence of every state in the area and their right to live in peace within secure and recognized boundaries free from threats or acts of force.'

* * *

John Scali, U.S. Permanent Representative to the UN,
Statement to the UN Security Council, July 14, 1973

"...What were the essential elements with which we began the search for peace in 1967?
"First, it is important to remember that the Council, in calling for a cease-fire to end the fighting in June 1967, did not address the question of who was responsible for the outbreak of that fighting. Nor did it call for unconditional Israeli withdrawal.
"Second, it is important to remember the nature and essential elements of Resolution 242 as they were generally understood at the time. The resolution was the result of compromise. Resolution 242 did not define the terms of

settlement. In the language of the resolution itself, it defined a set of 'provisions and principles' which constitute a framework for the terms of a final settlement. It is only fair to note that the terms to be negotiated must therefore be consistent with those provisions and principles—not just with some of them, but with all of them taken together. If the terms of a settlement do not meet that test, they cannot, in our view, form part of the just and lasting peace we seek. Too often one side or the other has sought to emphasize certain elements of Resolution 242 while ignoring others.

"What are the main provisions and principles of Resolution 242?

"First, it includes in its preamble 'the inadmissibility of the acquisition of territory by war and the need to work for a just and lasting peace in which every State in the area can live in security.' We accept this principle as important and significant.

"Second, Resolution 242 affirms that peace should include the application of two coequal principles. One is 'Withdrawal of Israeli armed forces from territories occupied' in the 1967 conflict. My government endorses that principle in the context of the resolution as a whole. But the principle of withdrawal cannot be separated from the next balancing paragraph, which affirmed the principle of 'Termination of all claims or states of belligerency and respect for and acknowledgment of the sovereignty, territorial integrity and political independence of every state in the area and their right to live in peace within secure and recognized boundaries free from threats or acts of force.'

"Third, Resolution 242 affirms the necessity for guaranteeing freedom of navigation and for guaranteeing the territorial inviolability and political independence of every state in the area. Clearly the specific measures by which these important interests of the parties are to be guaranteed must be part of the detailed terms of a final settlement. They must be part of the structure of peace.

"Fourth, Resolution 242 affirms the necessity for achieving a just settlement of the refugee problem. That, too, must clearly be part of the structure of peace. My government has made clear on a number of occasions our view that no structure of peace in the Middle East can be just and lasting if it does not make provision for the legitimate aspirations of the Palestinians. In our view, it is for the parties to work out what this means in specific terms.

"Finally, Resolution 242 calls for agreement. In the context of the resolution, this clearly means agreement between the parties concerned. Ambassador [Gunnar] Jarring, to whom I wish to pay special tribute today, was subsequently selected to assist the parties to this end. My government has never seen how such agreement is possible without an ongoing, serious, negotiating process, either direct or indirect, which engages the parties themselves. We believe each member of this Council should do everything possible to encourage the parties to engage in such a dialogue. The recess in these deliberations which now lies before us provides each and all of us with an opportunity to take stock and to consider what can be done to bring about forward movement.

"In the days just passed, several speakers have attributed to the United States a certain partisanship in its view of the Arab-Israeli dispute. Perhaps in doing so, these speakers were reflecting a certain partisanship of their own. In any case, I wish to dismiss these allegations without exception. Like my predecessors, I represent to the best of my ability the interest of the Unites States, and not those of any other single state. In the Middle East, the overriding interest of the U.S. is in peace—a peace that will end the fear and uncertainty of the past quarter century. The interest of the United States demands we press ahead to seek that peace—a peace that will allow Arab and Israeli alike to reside within secure and recognized boundaries. The United States urgently desires friendly and enduring relations with all countries of the Middle East.

"In his recent report to Congress, President Nixon solemnly stated, '...I have said that no other crisis area of the world has greater importance or higher priority for the United States in the second term of my administration.' Mr. President, that judgment and that resolve are unchanged.

"Our determination to serve this interest has only been strengthened by the passage of time. The disappointments of the past have strengthened the imperative to seek peace. Neither the United States nor any other power or combination of powers can negotiate such a peace. Only the parties can do that. But let there be no doubt about our determination to contribute whatever we can to the creation of circumstances in which the parties can achieve peace and security through negotiations.

"We note, as other speakers before us have done, that in today's world, security means more than territory, more than the hoarding of armaments, and more than merely the absence of belligerency. Security—real security for all parties—depends on willingness to put aside bitter quarrels, prejudices, fears, and misapprehensions of the past and to look ahead positively to developing a broad range of mutual interests which gives each party a vested interest in preserving peace.

"What are the key issues with which such negotiations must come to grips? In simplest terms they are the issues of sovereignty and security. The parties must find a way to reconcile the two. One aspect of this problem is the question of boundaries. There are many strongly held views about where final boundaries between Israel and its neighbors should be drawn. Resolution 242 has often been cited to support one view or another. But the fact is that Resolution 242 is silent on the specific question of where the final border should be located. It neither endorses nor precludes— let me repeat, neither endorses nor precludes—the armistice lines which existed between Israel, Egypt, Jordan, and Syria on June 4, 1967, as the final secure and recognized boundaries. Everyone knew when Resolution 242 was approved that this was an area of ambiguity. This was part of the compromise to which I have referred.

"The central message of Resolution 242 is that there should be a fundamental change in the nature of the relationship of the parties with each other, a change from belligerency to peace, from insecurity to security, from dispossession and despair to hope and dignity for the Palestinians. Let me say again: it seems clear to us—logically, politically, historically, realistically—that the question of agreement of final boundaries must be viewed in the context of the total thrust and intent of Resolution 242. This question must therefore be resolved as part of the process of reaching agreement on all the complex factors governing a new relationship among the parties to replace that defined in the 1949 armistice agreements.

"Mr. President, I have recalled the history of our efforts in 1967 not to argue the past, but because I believe we need to restore our perspective as we look to the future. Many sincere efforts have been made, by Ambassador Jarring and by governments, including my own, to help the parties find a way to negotiate the detailed terms of a final peace agreement. Whatever may have been their merits, none succeeded. We are therefore left with Resolution 242 as the only basis thus far accepted by both sides, with regard both to substance and to procedure. The principal parties concerned have accepted that basis, each in its own way, and this is what makes it uniquely important..."

* * *

Alfred L. Atherton, Jr., Assistant Secretary of State for Near East and South Asian Affairs, "A Status Report on the Peace Process," address to the Atlanta Foreign Policy Conference on U.S. interests in the Middle East, April 5, 1978

"... In six days Israel not only proved beyond all doubt that it was there to stay, but it also ended up occupying

Arab territory stretching to the Golan Heights of Syria, the Jordan River and the Suez Canal. Slowly, meticulously, painfully, the United States and other, like-minded members of the international community working with the parties to the conflict in the months immediately following the war, launched intensive diplomatic efforts to translate this new situation into the long-sought basis for genuine peace negotiations.

"The result was United Nations Security Council Resolution 242, adopted unanimously by the Council in November 1967. Here for the first time in twenty years was spelled out the framework for a settlement of the Arab-Israeli conflict. That resolution was and remains the basis for all the peacemaking efforts over the past decade. At its heart is a very simple formula: In return for Israeli withdrawal from territories occupied in the 1967 conflict, the Arabs will recognize Israel within a framework of peace and security agreed by both. It calls for a just and lasting peace based upon the right of every state in the area to live in peace within secure and recognized boundaries and upon Israeli withdrawal from territories occupied in 1967. Resolution 242 is clearly a package. The parts are linked together to make a balanced whole, to be carried out together or not at all.

"That having been said, let me note what Resolution 242 does not do. It does not define secure and recognized boundaries. It does not call for withdrawal from 'all' occupied territories or 'the' occupied territories. It does not require Israel to give up every inch of occupied territory. Neither, however, does it preclude Israeli withdrawal to the lines of 1967. In the final analysis, this issue can only be resolved in agreements negotiated by the parties. The emphasis of Resolution 242 taken as a whole, however, is clear. The emphasis is on establishing conditions of peace and security based upon the concept of withdrawal for peace. It is also clear that all the principles of Resolution 242, including the principle of withdrawal, were intended by its authors, and understood at the time by all the governments concerned, to apply wherever territory was occupied in 1967. In other words, the withdrawal-for-peace formula applies to all fronts of the conflict."

* * *

Vice President Walter Mondale
Address to the Israeli Knesset, July 2, 1978

"Resolution 242 is an equation. On the one hand, it recognizes the right of every state in the area to live in peace within secure and recognized borders free from threats or acts of force. We believe such a peace must include binding commitments to normal relations. In return, Israel would withdraw from territories occupied in the 1967 war. We believe the exact boundaries must be determined through negotiations by the parties themselves. They are not determined by Resolution 242.

"But these principles of 242 cannot be viewed in isolation or applied selectively. Together they form a fair and balanced formula and still the best basis for negotiating a peace between Israel and [its] neighbors...."

* * *

Harold Saunders, Assistant Secretary of State for Near East and South Asian Affairs,
World Affairs Council of Boston, January 29, 1979

"...It is essential to understand that the Camp David agreements are deeply rooted in the only basis for negotiation that has been agreed upon by all parties to the conflict—Resolution 242, adopted unanimously by the UN Security Council in November 1967.

"While there have been differences in interpretation of this resolution, at its heart Resolution 242 contains a very simple formula: In return for Israel's withdrawal from territories occupied in the 1967 conflict, the Arab states will recognize Israel within a framework of true peace and security agreed by all. Resolution 242 calls for a just and lasting peace based upon the right of every state in the area to live in peace within secure and recognized boundaries and upon Israeli withdrawal from territories occupied in 1967. Resolution 242 was clearly intended as a package. The parts are linked together to make a balanced whole, to be carried out together.

"That being said, let me note what Resolution 242 does not do.

"It does not define secure and recognized boundaries. It does not require Israel to give up every inch of occupied territory. Neither does it preclude Israeli withdrawal to the lines of 1967.

"Resolution 242 does not deal fully with the important Palestinian issue. No solution can be complete that does not recognize the aspirations of the Palestinian people for an identity of their own. President Carter recognized this in the early days of his Administration when he spoke of the need for a homeland for the Palestinians.

"Against this background, it should be understood that the Camp David framework does not supersede Resolution 242 but is firmly based upon it and serves to make more explicit some principles left by 242 to the negotiating process. In addition, it supplements Resolution 242 in spelling out the political dimensions of a settlement of the Palestinian issue."

***

President Ronald Reagan, Address to the Nation, September 1, 1982

"...The time has come for a new realism on the part of all the peoples of the Middle East. The State of Israel is an accomplished fact; it deserves unchallenged legitimacy within the community of nations. But Israel's legitimacy has thus far been recognized by too few countries, and has been denied by every Arab state except Egypt. Israel exists. It has a right to exist in peace, behind secure and defensible borders, and it has a right to demand of its neighbors that they recognize those facts.

"I have personally followed and supported Israel's heroic struggle for survival ever since the founding of the State of Israel thirty-four years ago. In the pre-1967 borders, Israel was barely ten miles wide at its narrowest point. The bulk of Israel's population lived within artillery range of hostile Arab armies. I am not about to ask Israel to live that way again...

"...We base our approach squarely on the principle that the Arab-Israeli conflict should be resolved through negotiation involving an exchange of territory for peace. This exchange is enshrined in UN Security Council Resolution 242, which is, in turn, incorporated in all its parts in the Camp David agreements. UN Resolution 242 remains wholly valid as the foundation stone of America's Middle East peace effort.

"It is the United States' position that, in return for peace, the withdrawal provision of Resolution 242 applies to all fronts, including the West Bank and Gaza. When the border is negotiated between Jordan and Israel our view on the extent to which Israel should be asked to give up territory will be heavily affected by the extent of true peace and normalization, and the security arrangements offered in return..."

* * *

George P. Shultz, Secretary of State,
Testimony to the Senate Foreign Relations Committee, September 10, 1982

"...The Camp David accords provide that these negotiated arrangements on final status must be 'just, comprehensive,... durable,' and 'based on Security Council

Resolutions 242 and 338 in all their parts.' Security Council Resolution 242 sets forth the two key principles:
  "(i) Withdrawal of Israeli armed forces from territories occupied...
  "(ii) Termination of all claims or states of belligerency and respect for and acknowledgment of the sovereignty, territorial integrity and political independence of every state in the area and their right to live in peace within secure and recognized boundaries free from threats or acts of force.
  "As it has often been summarized, peace for territory.
  "We believe these principles apply on all fronts, but our position on the extent of withdrawal will be significantly influenced by the extent and nature of the peace and security arrangements being offered in return..."

Interview in Amman, Jordan, April 5, 1988

"...It doesn't seem to me in the cards to think that you can just go back to the 1967 borders. In our proposal, we say Resolution 242 applies in each negotiation. And so obviously the question of territorial compromise is put into play by that. But that's what the negotiation has to be about: What is the nature of the compromise, and how will this work itself through?..."

Address to The Washington Institute, September 16, 1988

"...The objective is comprehensive peace between Israel and all its neighbors, achieved through negotiations based on United Nations Security Council Resolutions 242 and 338. This will require recognition that sovereignty cannot be defined in absolute terms. Today borders are porous. Openness is required for the free movement of ideas, people and goods. There will need to be a border demarcation, but not a wall established between peoples.

"The territorial issue needs to be addressed realistically. Israel will never negotiate from or return to the lines of partition or to the 1967 borders. But it must be prepared to withdraw—as Resolution 242 says—'from territories occupied in the recent conflict.' Peace and security for all sides are at stake..."

***

James Baker, Secretary of State
Press stakeout, White House, May 17, 1991

"Let me say something about 242 and 338... The parties with whom we've been talking have agreed that the objective is a comprehensive settlement based on 242 and 338. And that represents, I think, a pretty important agreement. That doesn't bring you to a peace conference, because you've got to get agreement on every last thing before you can have a peace conference. But that fundamental agreement has to be made, and it has been made."

Question: "But, Mr. Secretary, the parties don't even agree on what 242 and 338 require."

Mr. Baker: "If there was an agreement on what 242 required, you wouldn't have to have a conference. You wouldn't even, indeed, have to have negotiations. That's what the negotiations are for, to determine exactly what's meant by 242."

***

President George Bush, Address to Madrid peace conference, October 30, 1991

"... We come to Madrid on a mission of hope to begin work on a just, lasting and comprehensive settlement to the conflict in the Middle East. We come here to seek peace for a part of the world that in the long memory of man has known far too much hatred, anguish and war. I can think of no endeavor more worthy or more necessary.

"Our objective must be clear and straightforward. It is not simply to end the state of war in the Middle East and replace it with a state of non-belligerency. This is not enough. This would not last. Rather, we seek peace. Real peace. And by real peace, I mean treaties, security, diplomatic relations, economic relations, trade, investment, cultural exchange, even tourism. What we seek is a Middle East where vast resources are no longer devoted to armaments; a Middle East where young people no longer have to dedicate and all too often give their lives to combat; a Middle East no longer victimized by fear and terror; a Middle East where normal men and women lead normal lives...

"...Peace in the Middle East need not be a dream. Peace is possible. The Egyptian-Israeli peace treaty is striking proof that former adversaries can make and sustain peace. And moreover, parties in the Middle East have respected agreements, not only in the Sinai, but on the Golan Heights as well. The fact that we are all gathered here today for the first time attests to a new potential for peace. Each of us has taken an important step toward real peace by meeting here in Madrid. All the formulas on paper, all the pious declarations in the world, won't bring peace if there is no practical mechanism for moving ahead.

"Peace will only come as the result of direct negotiations, compromise, give-and-take. Peace cannot be imposed from the outside by the United States or anyone else. And while we will continue to do everything possible to help the parties overcome obstacles, peace must come from within. We come here to Madrid as realists. We don't expect peace to be negotiated in a day or a week or a month or even a year. It will take time. Indeed, it should take time—time for parties so long at war to learn to talk to one another, to listen to one another, time to heal old wounds and build trust. In this quest, time need not be the enemy of progress.

"What we envision is a process of direct negotiations proceeding along two tracks, one between Israel and the Arab states, the other between Israel and the Palestinians. Negotiations are to be conducted on the basis of UN Security Council Resolutions 242 and 338. The real work will not happen here in the plenary sessions but in direct, bilateral negotiations. This conference cannot impose a settlement on the participants or veto agreements. And just as important, the conference can only be reconvened with the consent of every participant.

"Progress is in the hands of the parties who must live with the consequences. Soon after the bilateral talks commence, parties will convene as well to organize multilateral negotiations. These will focus on issues that cross national boundaries and are common to the region—arms control, water, refugee concerns, economic development. Progress in these fora is not intended as a substitute for what must be decided in the bilateral talks. To the contrary, progress in the multilateral issues can help create atmosphere in which long-standing bilateral disputes can more easily be settled.

"For Israel and the Palestinians, a framework already exists for diplomacy. Negotiations will be conducted in phases, beginning with talks on interim self-government arrangements. We aim to reach agreement within one year; and once agreed, interim self-government arrangements will last for five years. Beginning the third year, negotiations will commence on permanent status.

"No one can say with any precision what the end result will be. In our view, something must be developed, something acceptable to Israel, the Palestinians and Jordan, that gives the Palestinian people meaningful control over their own lives and fate and provides for the acceptance and security of Israel. We can all appreciate that both Israelis and Palestinians are worried about compromise, worried about compromising even the smallest point, for fear it becomes a precedent for what really matters. But no one should avoid compromise on interim arrangements for a simple reason. Nothing agreed to now will prejudice permanent status negotiations. To the contrary, these subsequent negotiations will be determined on their own merits.

"Peace cannot depend upon promises alone. Real peace, lasting peace, must be based upon the security for all states and peoples, including Israel. For too long, the Israeli people have lived in fear, surrounded by an unaccepting Arab world. And now is the ideal moment for the Arab world to demonstrate that attitudes have changed, that the Arab world is willing to live in peace with Israel and make allowances for Israel's reasonable security needs. We know that peace must also be based on fairness. In the absence of fairness, there will be no legitimacy, no stability. And this applies above all to the Palestinian people, many of whom have known turmoil and frustration above all else.

"Israel now has an opportunity to demonstrate that it is willing to enter into a new relationship with its Palestinian neighbors, one predicated upon mutual respect and cooperation.

"Throughout the Middle East, we seek a stable and enduring settlement. We've not defined what this means. Indeed, I make these points with no map showing where the final borders are to be drawn. And nevertheless, we believe that territorial compromise is essential for peace. Boundaries should reflect the quality of both security and political arrangements, and the United States is prepared to accept whatever the parties themselves find acceptable. What we seek, as I said on March 6, is a solution that meets the twin tests of fairness and security. I know, I expect we all know, that these negotiations will not be easy. I know too, that these negotiations will not be smooth. There will be disagreement and criticism, setbacks—who knows, possibly interruptions. Negotiation and compromise are always painful.

"Success will escape us if we focus solely upon what is being given up. We must fix our vision on what real peace would bring. Peace, after all, means not just avoiding war and the cost of preparing for it. The Middle East is blessed with great resources—physical, financial, and yes, above all, human. And new opportunities are within reach if we only have the vision to embrace them. To succeed, we must recognize that peace is in the interest of all parties, war to the absolute advantage of none. The alternative to peace in the Middle East is a future of violence and waste and tragedy. In any future war lurks the dangers of weapons of mass destruction. As we learned in the Gulf War, modern arsenals make it possible to attack urban areas, to put the lives of innocent men, women, and children at risk, to transform city streets, schools, children's playgrounds into battlefields.

"Today we can decide to take a different path to the future: to avoid conflict. And I call upon all parties to avoid unilateral acts, be they words or deeds, that would invite retaliation or, worse yet, prejudice or even threaten the process itself. I call upon all parties to consider taking measures that will bolster mutual confidence and trust, steps that signal a sincere commitment to reconciliation..."

* * *

President Bill Clinton
Interview in Middle East Insight, November-December 1992

"The most noticeable change [in the peace talks] is the election in Israel of Prime Minister Rabin, who has wasted no time in breathing new life into the negotiations. Israel has reaffirmed its recognition of those UN resolutions that are the foundation of the peace process, and has specifically applied them to the negotiations with Syria.

"The Rabin government has also curbed settlements and taken other measures to build confidence in relations with the Palestinians and other Arab parties. Now I think it's time for the Arabs to make more moves toward Israel."

Question: "You mean a move like Egypt's President Sadat made in 1977, when he journeyed to Jerusalem?"

President Clinton: "Or something else that would have that kind of dramatic effect. For example, at least one of the Arab countries should break the ice and end the boycott against Israel. That would be the best thing they could do. If several Arab countries decided to do that, in response to some of the moves Israel has made, then I think we'd be well on our way to negotiating an agreement consistent with UN Resolution 242 and the Camp David Accords."

Statement at Joint White House Press Stakeout with Yitzhak Rabin, March 15, 1993

"We focused today on our common objective of turning 1993 into a year of peacemaking in the Middle East. Prime Minister Rabin has made clear to me today that pursuing peace with security is his highest mission. I have pledged that my administration will be active in helping the parties to achieve that end.

"At the same time, Prime Minister Rabin and I agree that our common objectives should be real, lasting, just, and comprehensive peace based on Resolutions 242 and 338. It must involve full normalization, diplomatic relations, open borders, commerce, tourism—the human bonds that are both the fruits and the best guarantee of peace. And Israel's security must be assured. The Israeli people cannot be expected to make peace unless they come to know real peace.

"Those, like Prime Minister Rabin, who genuinely seek peace in the Middle East, will find in me and my administration a full partner. But those who seek to subvert the peace process will find zero tolerance here for their deplorable acts of violence and terrorism. Prime Minister Rabin has told me that he is prepared to take risks for peace. He has told his own people the same thing. I have told him that our role is to help to minimize those risks. We will do that by further reinforcing our commitment to maintaining Israel's qualitative military edge."

***

Edward Djerejian, Assistant Secretary of State for Near East and South Asian Affairs
Testimony before the Foreign Operations Subcommittee of the House Appropriations Committee, March 8, 1993

"The United States remains committed to the process of peacemaking launched at Madrid, including the terms of reference for negotiations and the letters of assurances provided by the U.S. government to each party. Our policy remains directed at the achievement of a comprehensive Arab-Israeli peace settlement based on UN Security Council Resolutions 242 and 338. The United States is prepared to play an active role to help narrow and overcome substantive differences along the lines I indicated earlier.

"In playing this role Secretary Christopher characterized as 'full partner,' he stressed that in no way would we substitute ourselves for the parties themselves, but, rather, we would assist the parties who are engaged in direct face-to-face negotiations as an active intermediary, an honest broker, a facilitator in helping to move the talks forward and to narrow substantive differences.

"... I have learned—painfully—never to use the word 'optimism' in terms of the Arab-Israeli conflict and resolution, but I certainly can say that during the course of the Arab-Israeli negotiations since Madrid that real progress has been made in the negotiating tracks.

"Each one of the negotiating tracks—the Israeli-Syrian, the Israeli-Lebanese, the Israeli-Palestinian, and the Israeli-Jordanian—has been involved in the core issues of land, peace, and security, which are really at the heart of the Arab-Israeli peace process. And each negotiating track goes its own pace with its own substantive issues."

SECTION C

SELECTED DOCUMENTS

THE CAMP DAVID ACCORDS

September 17, 1978

A FRAMEWORK FOR PEACE IN THE MIDDLE EAST AGREED AT CAMP DAVID

Mohammed Anwar al-Sadat, President of the Arab Republic of Egypt, and Menachem Begin, Prime Minister of Israel, met with Jimmy Carter, President of the United States of America, at Camp David from September 5 to September 17, 1978, and have agreed on the following framework for peace in the Middle East. They invite other parties to the Arab-Israeli conflict to adhere to it.

Preamble
The search for peace in the Middle East must be guided by the following:

• The agreed basis for a peaceful settlement of the conflict between Israel and its neighbors is United Nations Security Council Resolution 242, in all its parts.

• After four wars during thirty years, despite intensive human efforts, the Middle East, which is the cradle of civilization and the birthplace of three great religions, does not yet enjoy the blessings of peace. The people of the Middle East yearn for peace so that the vast human and natural resources of the region can be turned to the pursuits of peace and so that this area can become a model for coexistence and cooperation among nations.

- The historic initiative of President Sadat in visiting Jerusalem and the reception accorded to him by the Parliament, government and people of Israel, and the reciprocal visit of Prime Minister Begin to Ismailia, the peace proposals made by both leaders, as well as the warm reception of these missions by the peoples of both countries, have created an unprecedented opportunity for peace which must not be lost if this generation and future generations are to be spared the tragedies of war.

- The provisions of the Charter of the United Nations and the other accepted norms of international law and legitimacy now provide accepted standards for the conduct of relations among all states.

- To achieve a relationship of peace, in the spirit of Article 2 of the United Nations Charter, future negotiations between Israel and any neighbor prepared to negotiate peace and security with it, are necessary for the purpose of carrying out all the provisions and principles of Resolutions 242 and 338.

- Peace requires respect for the sovereignty, territorial integrity and political independence of every state in the area and their right to live in peace within secure and recognized boundaries free from threats or acts of force. Progress toward that goal can accelerate movement toward a new era of reconciliation in the Middle East marked by cooperation in promoting economic development, in maintaining stability, and in assuring security.

- Security is enhanced by a relationship of peace and by cooperation between nations which enjoy normal relations. In addition, under the terms of peace treaties, the parties can, on the basis of reciprocity, agree to special security arrangements such as demilitarized zones, limited armaments areas, early warning stations, the presence of international forces, liaison, agreed measures for monitoring, and other arrangements that they agree are useful.

Framework
Taking these factors into account, the parties are determined to reach a just, comprehensive, and durable settlement of the Middle East conflict through the conclusion of peace treaties based on Security Council Resolutions 242 and 338 in all their parts. Their purpose is to achieve peace and good neighborly relations. They recognize that, for peace to endure, it must involve all those who have been most deeply affected by the conflict. They therefore agree that this framework as appropriate is intended by them to constitute a basis for peace not only between Egypt and Israel, but also between Israel and each of its other neighbors which is prepared to negotiate peace with Israel on this basis. With that objective in mind, they have agreed to proceed as follows:

A. West Bank and Gaza
1. Egypt, Israel, Jordan and the representatives of the Palestinian people should participate in negotiations on the resolution of the Palestinian problem in all its aspects. To achieve that objective, negotiations relating to the West Bank and Gaza should proceed in three stages:

(a) Egypt and Israel agree that, in order to ensure a peaceful and orderly transfer of authority, and taking into account the security concerns of all the parties, there should be transitional arrangements for the West Bank and Gaza for a period not exceeding five years. In order to provide full autonomy to the inhabitants, under these arrangements the Israeli military government and its civilian administration will be withdrawn as soon as a self-governing authority has been freely elected by the inhabitants of these areas to replace the existing military government. To negotiate the details of a transitional arrangement, the Government of Jordan will be invited to join the negotiations on the basis of this framework. These new arrangements should give due consideration both to the principle of self-government by the inhabitants of these territories and to the legitimate security concerns of the parties involved.

(b) Egypt, Israel, and Jordan will agree on the modalities for establishing the elected self-governing authority in the West Bank and Gaza. The delegations of Egypt and Jordan may include Palestinians from the West Bank and Gaza or other Palestinians as mutually agreed. The parties will negotiate an agreement which will define the powers and responsibilities of the self-governing authority to be exercised in the West Bank and Gaza. A withdrawal of Israeli armed forces will take place and there will be a redeployment of the remaining Israeli forces into specified security locations. The agreement will also include arrangements for assuring internal and external security and public order. A strong local police force will be established, which may include Jordanian citizens. In addition, Israeli and Jordanian forces will participate in joint patrols and in the manning of control posts to assure the security of the borders.

(c) When the self-governing authority (administrative council) in the West Bank and Gaza is established and inaugurated, the transitional period of five years will begin. As soon as possible, but not later than the third year after the beginning of the transitional period, negotiations will take place to determine the final status of the West Bank and Gaza and its relationship with its neighbors, and to conclude a peace treaty between Israel and Jordan by the end of the transitional period. These negotiations will be conducted among Egypt, Israel, Jordan, and the elected representatives of the inhabitants of the West Bank and Gaza. Two separate but related committees will be convened, one committee, consisting of representatives of the four parties which will negotiate and agree on the final status of the West Bank and Gaza, and its relationship with its neighbors, and the second committee, consisting of representatives of Israel and representatives of Jordan to be joined by the elected representatives of the inhabitants of the West Bank and Gaza, to negotiate the peace treaty between Israel and Jordan, taking into account the agreement reached on the final status of the West Bank and Gaza. The negotiations shall be based on all the provisions and principles of UN Security Council Resolution 242. The negotiations will resolve, among other matters, the location of the boundaries and the nature of the security arrangements. The solution from the negotiations must also recognize the legitimate rights of the Palestinian people and their just requirements. In this way, the Palestinians will participate in the determination of their own future through:

(1) The negotiations among Egypt, Israel, Jordan and the representatives of the inhabitants of the West Bank and Gaza to agree on the final status of the West Bank and Gaza and other outstanding issues by the end of the transitional period.

(2) Submitting their agreement to a vote by the elected representatives of the inhabitants of the West Bank and Gaza.

(3) Providing for the elected representatives of the inhabitants of the West Bank and Gaza to decide how they shall govern themselves consistent with the provisions of their agreement.

(4) Participating as stated above in the work of the committee negotiating the peace treaty between Israel and Jordan.

2. All necessary measures will be taken and provisions made to assure the security of Israel and its neighbors during the transitional period and beyond. To assist in providing such security, a strong local police force will be constituted by the self-governing authority. It will be composed of inhabitants of the West Bank and Gaza. The police will maintain continuing liaison on internal security matters with the designated Israeli, Jordanian, and Egyptian officers.

3. During the transitional period, representatives of Egypt, Israel, Jordan, and the self-governing authority will constitute a continuing committee to decide by agreement on the modalities of admission of persons displaced from the West Bank and Gaza in 1967, together with necessary measures to prevent disruption and disorder. Other matters of common concern may also be dealt with by this committee.

4. Egypt and Israel will work with each other and with other interested parties to establish agreed procedures for a prompt, just and permanent implementation of the resolution of the refugee problem.

B. *Egypt-Israel*

1. Egypt and Israel undertake not to resort to the threat or the use of force to settle disputes. Any disputes shall be settled by peaceful means in accordance with the provisions of Article 33 of the Charter of the United Nations.

2. In order to achieve peace between them, the parties agree to negotiate in good faith with a goal of concluding within three months from the signing of the Framework a peace treaty between them while inviting the other parties to the conflict to proceed simultaneously to negotiate and conclude similar peace treaties with a view to achieving a comprehensive peace in the area. The

Framework for the Conclusion of a Peace Treaty between Egypt and Israel will govern the peace negotiations between them. The parties will agree on the modalities and the timetable for the implementation of their obligations under the treaty.

C. *Associated Principles*

1. Egypt and Israel state that the principles and provisions described below should apply to peace treaties between Israel and each of its neighbors—Egypt, Jordan, Syria and Lebanon.

2. Signatories shall establish among themselves relationships normal to states at peace with one another. To this end, they should undertake to abide by all the provisions of the charter of the United Nations. Steps to be taken in this respect include:

(a) full recognition;
(b) abolishing economic boycotts;
(c) guaranteeing that under their jurisdiction the citizens of the other parties shall enjoy the protection of the due process of law.

3. Signatories should explore possibilities for economic development in the context of final peace treaties, with the objective of contributing to the atmosphere of peace, cooperation and friendship which is their common goal.

4. Claims Commissions may be established for the mutual settlement of all financial claims.

5. The United States shall be invited to participate in the talks on matters related to the modalities of the implementation of the agreements and working out the timetable for the carrying out of the obligation of the parties.

6. The United Nations Security Council shall be requested to endorse the peace treaties and ensure that their provisions shall not be violated. The permanent members of the Security Council shall be requested to underwrite the peace treaties and ensure respect for their provisions. They shall also be requested to conform their policies and actions with the undertakings contained in this Framework.

For the Government of the Arab Republic of Egypt:
A. Sadat

For the Government of the Israel:
M. Begin

Witnessed by:
Jimmy Carter,
President of the United States of America

FRAMEWORK FOR THE CONCLUSION OF A PEACE TREATY BETWEEN EGYPT AND ISRAEL

In order to achieve peace between them, Israel and Egypt agree to negotiate in good faith with a goal of concluding within three months of the signing of this framework a peace treaty between them.

It is agreed that:

The site of the negotiations will be under a United Nations flag at a location or locations to be mutually agreed.

All of the principles of UN Resolution 242 will apply in this resolution of the dispute between Israel and Egypt.

Unless otherwise mutually agreed, terms of the peace treaty will be implemented between two and three years after the peace treaty is signed.

The following matters are agreed between the parties:

(a) the full exercise of Egyptian sovereignty up to the internationally recognized border between Egypt and mandated Palestine;

(b) the withdrawal of Israeli armed forces from the Sinai;

(c) the use of airfields left by the Israelis near El Arish, Rafah, Ras en Naqb, and Sharm el Sheikh for civilian purposes only, including possible commercial use by all nations;

(d) the right of free passage by ships of Israel through the Gulf of Suez and the Suez Canal on the basis of the Constantinople Convention of 1888 applying to all nations; the Strait of Tiran and the Gulf of Aqaba are international waterways to be open to all nations for unimpeded and nonsuspendable freedom of navigation and overflight;

(e) the construction of a highway between the Sinai and Jordan near Eilat with guaranteed free and peaceful passage by Egypt and Jordan; and

(f) the stationing of military forces listed below.

Stationing Of Forces

A. No more than one division (mechanized or infantry) of Egyptian armed forces will be stationed within an area lying approximately 50 kilometers (km) east of the Gulf of Suez and the Suez Canal.

B. Only United Nations forces and civil police equipped with light weapons to perform normal police functions will be stationed within an area lying west of the international border and the Gulf of Aqaba, varying in width from 20 km to 40 km.

C. In the area within 3 km east of the international border there will be Israeli limited military forces not to exceed four infantry battalions and United Nations observers.

D. Border patrol units, not to exceed three battalions, will supplement the civil police in maintaining order in the area not included above.

The exact demarcation of the above areas will be as decided during the peace negotiations.

Early warning stations may exist to insure compliance with the terms of the agreement.

United Nations forces will be stationed: (a) in part of the area in the Sinai lying within about 20 km of the Mediterranean Sea and adjacent to the international border, and (b) in the Sharm el Sheikh are to ensure freedom of passage through the Straits of Tiran; and these forces will not be removed unless such removal is approved by the Security Council of the United Nations with a unanimous vote of the five permanent members.

After a peace treaty is signed, and after the interim withdrawal is complete, normal relations will be established between Egypt and Israel, including: full recognition, including diplomatic, economic and cultural relations; termination of economic boycotts and barriers to the free movement of goods and people; and mutual protection of citizens by the due process of law.

Interim Withdrawal

Between three months and nine months after the signing of the peace treaty, all Israeli forces will withdraw east of a line extending from a point east of El Arish to Ras Muhammad, the exact location of this line to be determined by mutual agreement.

For the Government of the Arab Republic of Egypt:
A. Sadat

For the Government of Israel:
M. Begin

Witnessed by:
Jimmy Carter
President of the United States of America

TREATY OF PEACE BETWEEN THE ARAB REPUBLIC OF EGYPT AND THE STATE OF ISRAEL

March 26, 1979

The Government of the Arab Republic of Egypt and the Government of the State of Israel:

Preamble
Convinced of the urgent necessity of the establishment of a just, comprehensive and lasting peace in the Middle East in accordance with Security Council Resolutions 242 and 338;

Reaffirming their adherence to the "Framework for Peace in the Middle East Agreed at Camp David," dated September 17, 1978;

Noting that the aforementioned Framework as appropriate is intended to constitute a basis for peace not only between Egypt and Israel but also between Israel and each of its other Arab neighbors which is prepared to negotiate peace with it on this basis;

Desiring to bring to an end the state of war between them and to establish a peace in which every state in the area can live in security;

Convinced that the conclusion of a Treaty of Peace between Egypt and Israel is an important step in the search for comprehensive peace in the area and for the attainment of the settlement of the Arab-Israeli conflict in all its aspects;

Inviting the other Arab parties to this dispute to join the peace process with Israel guided by and based on the principles of the aforementioned Framework;

Desiring as well to develop friendly relations and cooperation between themselves in accordance with the United Nations Charter and the principles of international law governing international relations in times of peace;

Agree to the following provisions in the free exercise of their sovereignty, in order to implement the "Framework for the Conclusion of a Peace Treaty Between Egypt and Israel":

Article I

1. The state of war between the Parties will be terminated and peace will be established between them upon the exchange of instruments of ratification of this Treaty.

2. Israel will withdraw all its armed forces and civilians from the Sinai behind the international boundary between Egypt and mandated Palestine, as provided in the annexed protocol (Annex I), and Egypt will resume the exercise of its full sovereignty over the Sinai.

3. Upon completion of the interim withdrawal provided for in Annex I, the Parties will establish normal and friendly relations, in accordance with Article III (3).

Article II

The permanent boundary between Egypt and Israel is the recognized international boundary between Egypt and the former mandated territory of Palestine, as shown in the map at Annex II, without prejudice to the issue of the status of the Gaza Strip. The parties recognize this boundary as inviolable. Each will respect the territorial integrity of the other, including their territorial waters and airspace.

Article III

1. The Parties will apply between them the provisions of the Charter of the United Nations and the principles of

international law governing relations among states in times of peace. In particular:

 a. They recognize and will respect each other's sovereignty, territorial integrity and political independence;

 b. They recognize and will respect each other's right to live in peace within their secure and recognized boundaries;

 c. They will refrain from the threat or use of force, directly or indirectly, against each other and will settle all disputes between them by peaceful means.

2. Each Party undertakes to ensure that acts or threats of belligerency, hostility, or violence do not originate from and are not committed from within its territory, or by any forces subject to its control or by any other forces stationed on its territory, against the population, citizens or property of the other Party. Each Party also undertakes to refrain from organizing, instigating, inciting, assisting or participating in acts or threats of belligerency, hostility, subversion or violence against the other Party, anywhere, and undertakes to ensure that perpetrators of such acts are brought to justice.

3. The Parties agree that the normal relationship established between them will include full recognition, diplomatic, economic and cultural relations, termination of economic boycotts and discriminatory barriers to the free movement of people and goods, and will guarantee the mutual enjoyment of citizens of the due process of law. The process by which they undertake to achieve such a relationship parallel to the implementation of other provisions of this treaty is set out in the annexed protocol (Annex III).

Article IV

1. In order to provide maximum security for both Parties on the basis of reciprocity, agreed security arrangements will be established including limited force zones in Egyptian and Israeli territory, and United Nations forces

and observers, described in detail as to nature and timing in Annex I, and other security arrangements the Parties may agree upon.

2. The Parties agree to the stationing of United Nations personnel in areas described in Annex I. The Parties agree not to request withdrawal of the United Nations personnel and that these personnel will not be removed unless such removal is approved by the Security Council of the United Nations, with the affirmative vote of the five Permanent Members, unless the Parties otherwise agree.

3. A Joint Commission will be established to facilitate the implementation of the Treaty, as provided for in Annex I.

4. The security arrangements provided for in paragraphs 1 and 2 of this Article may at the request of either party be reviewed and amended by mutual agreement of the Parties.

Article V

1. Ships of Israel, and cargoes destined for or coming from Israel, shall enjoy the right of free passage through the Suez Canal and its approaches through the Gulf of Suez and the Mediterranean Sea on the basis of the Constantinople Convention of 1888, applying to all nations. Israeli nationals, vessels and cargoes, as well as persons, vessels and cargoes destined for or coming from Israel, shall be accorded nondiscriminatory treatment in all matters connected with usage of the canal.

2. The Parties consider the Strait of Tiran and the Gulf of Aqaba to be international waterways open to all nations for unimpeded and nonsuspendable freedom of navigation and overflight. The Parties will respect each others' right to navigation and overflight for access to either country through the Strait of Tiran and the Gulf of Aqaba.

Article VI

1. This Treaty does not affect and shall not be interpreted as affecting in any way the rights and obligations of the Parties under the Charter of the United Nations.

2. The Parties undertake to fulfill in good faith their obligations under this Treaty, without regard to action or inaction of any other party and independently of any instrument external to this Treaty.

3. They further undertake to take all the necessary measures for the application in their relations of the provisions of the multilateral conventions to which they are parties, including the submission of appropriate notification to the Secretary-General of the United Nations and other depositories of such conventions.

4. The Parties undertake not to enter into any obligation in conflict with this Treaty.

5. Subject to Article 103 of the United Nations Charter, in the event of a conflict between the obligations of the Parties under the present Treaty and any of their other obligations, the obligations under this Treaty will be binding and implemented.

Article VII

1. Disputes arising out of the application or interpretation of this Treaty shall be resolved by negotiations.

2. Any such disputes which cannot be settled by negotiations shall be resolved by conciliation or submitted to arbitration.

Article VIII

The Parties agree to establish a claims commission for the mutual settlement of all financial claims.

Article IX

1. This Treaty shall enter into force upon exchange of instruments of ratification.[Egypt and Israel exchanged ratifications, April 25, 1979].

2. This Treaty supersedes the Agreement between Egypt and Israel of September, 1975.

3. All protocols, annexes, and maps attached to this Treaty shall be regarded as an integral part hereof.

4. The Treaty shall be communicated to the Secretary-General of the United Nations for registration in accordance with the provisions of Article 102 of the Charter of the United Nations.

Done at Washington, D.C. this 26th day of March, 1979, in triplicate in the English, Arabic, and Hebrew languages, each text being equally authentic. In case of any divergence of interpretation, the English text shall prevail.

For the Government of the Arab Republic of Egypt:
A. Sadat

For the Government of Israel:
M. Begin

INVITATION TO THE MADRID CONFERENCE

October 18, 1991

On behalf of President Gorbachev and President Bush, we are very pleased to convey the attached invitation. After extensive consultations with Israel, Arab States, and the Palestinians, we have concluded that an historic opportunity exists to advance the prospects for genuine peace throughout the region. The United States and the Soviet Union are deeply committed to helping the parties realize this opportunity.

We look forward to working with you closely in this historic endeavor, and count on your continuing support and active participation.

To facilitate preparations for the conference and ensuring negotiations we urgently request your positive response as soon as possible, but no later than 6:00 p.m. Washington time, October 23.

Sincerely,

James A. Baker III
Boris Dmirtyevich Pankin

INVITATION

After extensive consultations with Arab states, Israel and the Palestinians, the United States and the Soviet Union believe that an historic opportunity exists to advance the prospects for genuine peace throughout the region. The United States and the Soviet Union are prepared to assist the parties to achieve a just, lasting and comprehensive peace settlement, through direct negotiations along two tracks, between Israel and the Arab states, and between Israel and the Palestinians, based on United Nations Security Council Resolutions 242 and 338. The objective of this process is real peace.

Toward that end, the president of the U.S. and the president of the USSR invite you to a peace conference, which their countries will co-sponsor, followed immediately by direct negotiations. The conference will be convened in Madrid on October 30, 1991.

President Bush and President Gorbachev request your acceptance of this invitation no later than 6 p.m. Washington time, October 23, 1991, in order to ensure proper organization and preparation of the conference.

Direct bilateral negotiations will begin four days after the opening of the conference. Those parties who wish to attend multilateral negotiations will convene two weeks after the opening of the conference to organize those negotiations. The co-sponsors believe that those negotiations should focus on region-wide issues such as arms control and regional security, water, refugee issues, environment, economic development, and other subjects of mutual interest.

The co-sponsors will chair the conference which will be held at ministerial level. Governments to be invited include Israel, Syria, Lebanon and Jordan. Palestinians will be invited and attend as part of a joint Jordanian-Palestinian delegation. Egypt will be invited to the conference as a participant. The European Community will be a participant in the conference, alongside the United States and the Soviet Union and will be represented by its presidency. The Gulf Cooperation Council will be invited to send its secretary-general to the conference as an observer, and GCC member states will be invited to participate in organizing the negotiations on multilateral issues. The United Nations will be invited to send an observer, representing the secretary-general.

The conference will have no power to impose solutions on the parties or veto agreements reached by them. It will have no authority to make decisions for the parties and no ability to vote on issues or results. The conference can reconvene only with the consent of all the parties.

With respect to negotiations between Israel and Palestinians who are part of the joint Jordanian-Palestinian delegation, negotiations will be conducted with the objective of reaching agreement within one year. Once agreed the interim self-government arrangements will last for a period of five years, beginning the third year of the period of interim self-government arrangements, negotiations will take place on permanent status. These permanent status negotiations, and the negotiations between Israel and the Arab states, will take place on the basis of Resolutions 242 and 338.

It is understood that the co-sponsors are committed to making this process succeed. It is their intention to convene the conference and negotiations with those parties who agree to attend.

The co-sponsors believe that this process offers the promise of ending decades of confrontation and conflict and the hope of a lasting peace. Thus, the co-sponsors hope that the parties will approach these negotiations in a spirit of goodwill and mutual respect. In this way, the peace process can begin to break down the mutual suspicions and mistrust that perpetuate the conflict and allow the parties to begin to resolve their differences. Indeed, only through such a process can real peace and reconciliation among the Arab states, Israel and the Palestinians be achieved. And only through this process can the peoples of the Middle East attain the peace and security they richly deserve.

SECTION D

LEGAL INTERPRETATIONS

UNITED NATIONS SECURITY COUNCIL RESOLUTION 242 AND THE PROSPECTS FOR PEACE IN THE MIDDLE EAST

ARTHUR J. GOLDBERG[1]

(EXCERPTS)

The stated goal of Resolution 242 is the establishment of a just and lasting peace in which every State in the area can live in security. It carefully, and perhaps somewhat artfully, contains language which the adversaries cite in support of their respective and different positions. Israeli spokesmen point out that the Resolution expressly and by implication repudiates the concept of an imposed peace and opts, in the words of the Resolution, to achieve "agreement" and "a peaceful and accepted settlement."

Resolution 242, Israel says, in explicit terms rejects the long asserted claim of the Arab countries of the existence of a state of belligerency against Israel and its right to live in peace and security.

The Resolution calls for respect and acknowledgment of the sovereignty of every state in the area. Israel contends that, since it never denied the sovereignty of its neighboring countries, this language obviously requires these countries to acknowledge the sovereignty of Israel and its right to exist free from force or the threats of force.

---

[1] Reprinted with permission from Arthur J. Goldberg, "United Nations Security Council Resolution 242 and the Prospects for Peace in the Middle East," © *Columbia Journal of International Law*, volume 12, no. 2, 1973.

Here, too, the words of the Resolution support Israel's interpretation.

On the question of withdrawal, Israel points out that the Resolution does not explicitly require that Israel withdraw to the lines occupied by it on June 5, 1967, before the outbreak of the war. The Resolution, on this key question, Israel says, simply endorses the principle of "withdrawal of Israel armed forces from territories occupied in the recent conflict," and interrelates this with the principle that every state in the area is entitled to live in peace within "secure and recognized boundaries."

The notable omissions in regard to withdrawal, from Israel's viewpoint, are the words *all, the,* and the *June 5, 1967 lines.* The Israelis emphasize that there is lacking a declaration requiring Israel to withdraw from *all* of the territories occupied by it on and after *June 5, 1967.*

Further, Israel says that the presence of the secure and recognized boundary language demonstrates the necessity for border adjustments to ensure Israel's security, inasmuch as its boundaries were neither "secure" nor "recognized" under the armistice regime prior to the Six Day War.

The Arab nations, to buttress their claim that the Resolution calls for a complete Israeli withdrawal, say the Israeli interpretation of the Resolution's withdrawal language is overly restrictive. They point to the language of the Resolution emphasizing "the inadmissibility of the acquisition of territory by war" and "respect for and acknowledgment of the... territorial integrity... of every State in the area" This language, the Arab States argue, in effect, calls for complete withdrawal of Israeli forces from all the territories occupied by them in the Six Day War. In addition, the Arab States contend that the UN Charter itself in spirit supports their contention that military conquest of territory is inadmissible as a matter of international law.

Perhaps an objective conclusion from the withdrawal and related language of the Resolution is that the Resolution is ambiguous and neither commands nor prohibits territorial adjustments in the accepted and agreed upon peace agreements contemplated by the Resolution, although it "tilts" in favor of adjustments to ensure secure boundaries for Israel without endorsing the complete redrawing of the map of the Middle East. Moreover, the withdrawal language of the Resolution would seem to indicate that its patent ambiguities and the differing interpretations of the parties can only be resolved after negotiations of one kind or another between the parties.

On certain aspects, the Resolution is less ambiguous than its withdrawal language. Resolution 242 specifically calls for termination of all claims or states of belligerency and respect for and acknowledgment of the sovereignty of every State in the area. The Resolution also specifically endorses free passage through international waterways. In precise language it affirms "the necessity... [f]or guaranteeing freedom of navigation through international waterways in the area." With an end of belligerency, no good reason would exist under international law for denial to Israel of access to the Suez Canal and, particularly, to the Strait of Tiran.

The Resolution calls for "a just settlement of the refugee problem." It is of some significance that the Resolution does not reiterate the language of prior UN resolutions calling for total repatriation or optional compensation for these refugees, a concept long resisted by Israel. This would seem an implicit but realistic recognition that all must participate in solving this problem—Israel by a more generous policy of repatriation and compensation, the Arab States by a similar policy of encouraging resettlement in their vast lands, and the world community both by more generous financial assistance and liberal immigration policies.

The Resolution refers to the utility of the establishment of demilitarized zones in assuring peace and guaranteeing territorial inviolability. The location of the demilitarized zones is left, obviously, to the parties to negotiate.

Interestingly, all of the foregoing provisions of the Resolution are stated in preambulatory language or as principles or guidelines for a peace agreement. The only truly operative parts of the Resolution are the paragraphs requiring the Secretary General "to designate a Special Representative to proceed to the Middle East to establish and maintain contacts with the States concerned in order to promote agreement and assist efforts to achieve a peaceful and accepted settlement in accordance with the provisions and principles on this resolution," and requesting the Secretary General to report on the Special Representative's progress. It is this language which strongly supports the view that a peace settlement is not to be imposed and that the Resolution is not self-implementing. In fact, it is impossible to see how the Resolution, in light of its terms and ambiguities—which, by the way, were purposeful and not unintended—can be self-implementing. Rather, it seems inescapable that the Resolution contemplates that, with third party assistance, the parties are to negotiate in some way or another and to agree upon an acceptable settlement and agreement.

A most significant omission in the Resolution is any specific reference to the status of Jerusalem and the Resolution's failure to reaffirm past UN resolutions for the internationalization of the city. The logical inference from this omission is that 242 realistically recognizes the desuetude of the prior UN internationalization resolutions.

There is further light on the ambiguities of 242 in its legislative history. This history dates back to the very outbreak of the Six Day War. On the second day of the war, June 7, the UN Security Council, with the concurrence of Israel and Egypt (Syria later also agreed), unanimously voted a cease-fire. This cease-fire, however, was not conditioned upon the withdrawal of Israeli armed forces. They were, in effect, to stand in place, pending further developments. In UN history, this type of cease-fire is virtually unique. Generally, when a conflict breaks out, it is almost "boiler plate" for the United Nations to adopt a cease-fire resolution embracing withdrawal of the contending forces to the positions they occupied before the conflict.

The adoption of a simple cease-fire resolution in this situation was no accident. It arose from the fact that although the Arab States involved lost the war in its first few hours, they remained unwilling, at that time and considerably thereafter, to renounce belligerency, acknowledge Israel's right to exist as a sovereign state; and reopen the Strait of Tiran to Israel. In light of this position, the requisite majority of the UN Security Council was unwilling at the time to insist upon Israel's withdrawal as a condition for the cease-fire.

The legislative history also shows that the Security Council, in the first instance, and the Special Session of the General Assembly thereafter, were also unwilling by the required vote to condemn Israel as the aggressor in the Six Day War and to insist upon a withdrawal of Israeli forces before the conclusion of a peace agreement. A substantial number of UN members shared the view that President Nasser's actions in ousting the UN peacekeeping forces, in mobilizing his troops in the Sinai, and in closing the Gulf of Aqaba to Israeli shipping, were the prime causes of the war. As a consequence, the efforts of the Arab States, strongly supported by the Soviet Union, the Eastern bloc, and some other nations, for a condemnation of Israel as the aggressor and for its withdrawal to the June 5, 1967 lines, failed to command the requisite support either in the Security Council or in the Assembly. True, Israel also could not command the requisite majority for its position, but a standoff, not encompassing complete withdrawal, was obviously to its advantage.

There is another interesting chapter in the legislative history. The Arab States, during the Special Session of the General Assembly, rejected a compromise urged upon them by the Soviet Union because the compromise, *inter alia*, entailed the renunciation of belligerency and acknowledgment of Israel's right to exist as a sovereign nation with secure borders and with full access to the Suez Canal and the Gulf of Aqaba.

Why then did the Arab States subsequently accept Resolution 242, incorporating these principles, and why do they still profess acceptance of it? Why did Israel accept, and why does it still adhere to its acceptance, despite the Resolution's ambiguities and the differing interpretations of the Resolution voiced at the time of its adoption and since?

Having been rebuffed both in the Security Council and in the Assembly, the Arab States came to the conclusion that the language of the Resolution was the best they could hope for from the United Nations. They obviously counted on the Resolution's ambiguities to permit them to assert their own interpretation of the Resolution. They also relied heavily upon major Soviet support both diplomatically and militarily. Further, they conceived that the passage of time would erode the support of the United States and like-minded states for Israel.

To a certain extent, Arab calculations have been realized. World opinion, overwhelmingly supportive of Israel as the "underdog" at the time of the war, has, in some degree, shifted to a measure of sympathy for the defeated and now "underdog" Arab States. Some countries have watered down their prior support of the Resolution's principles. But the United States, despite some wavering, has not. It still remains the position of the United States that the way to peace in the Middle East is a negotiated peace agreement between the parties rather than the restoration of the prior and often breached armistice agreements. The United States continues to hope that the negotiations for a full settlement can be furthered by an interim one involving a limited withdrawal of Israeli forces from an area bordering on the Suez Canal. But this proposal, while acceptable to Israel, has thus far been rejected by Egypt.

An important element which may be conducive to a settlement is that the Soviet Union is not giving Egypt all the sophisticated hardware and offensive weaponry which it has requested. The Arab States, presumably, have learned that while the Soviet Union is willing to give them diplomatic and vocal support, it is not willing to risk a confrontation with the United States in their behalf.

The Israelis accepted Resolution 242, interestingly enough for some of the same reasons as their Arab antagonists. It was the best Israelis could hope to get from the United Nations under the given circumstances. They were rightfully fearful that the diplomatic support at that time would erode if they proved to be intransigent and demanded a complete vindication of their position. Like the Arab States, they concluded that the Resolution's ambiguities permitted them to assert their own interpretation of the Resolution. Despite inflammatory Soviet speechmaking, Israel was unwilling to provoke the Soviets unduly, fearing greater involvement by them in the area. Israel conceived that time would be on its side. Most important, in light of Israel's need for military hardware and economic assistance, the Israelis recognized the danger of alienating the United States government and American public opinion by an overly inflexible position.

Despite the passage of time since the adoption of Resolution 242, and perhaps because of it, I adhere to the view that the Resolution does provide the basis to achieve a peaceful and accepted settlement between the parties, provided they have and share the will and courage to achieve a just and lasting peace, which is the goal of the Resolution. Perhaps my "optimism" is based on the fact that the Resolution gives something to both sides.

LEGAL ASPECTS OF THE SEARCH FOR PEACE IN THE MIDDLE EAST

EUGENE V. ROSTOW[1]

(EXCERPTS)

I shall start, if I may, with Security Council Resolution No. 242, of November 22, 1967, for I consider it to be primary. That resolution was achieved after more than five months of intensive diplomatic effort on the part of the United States, Great Britain, Denmark, Canada, and a number of other countries. The history of that effort gives the text a very plain meaning indeed.

It will be recalled that when large-scale hostilities erupted on June 5, 1967, the Soviet Union blocked American cease-fire proposals for several days, until it realized what was happening in the field. Then, when the Cease-Fire Resolutions were finally in place, a major diplomatic campaign, extending around the world, was brought into focus first in the Security Council; then in the General Assembly; then at Glassboro; and finally back in the Security Council.

A number of positions emerged. Their interplay, and the resolution of that interplay, is reflected in the resolution itself.

---

[1] Reprinted with permission from Eugene V. Rostow, "Legal Interpretations of the Search for Peace in the Middle East," 64 ASIL PROC. 64 (1970), © The American Society of International Law.

The Soviet Union and its chief Arab associates wished to have Israel declared the aggressor and required, under Chapter VII if possible, to withdraw to the Armistice Demarcation Lines as they stood on June 5th, in exchange for the fewest possible assurances[1]: that after withdrawal Israeli maritime rights in the Strait of Tiran would be "no problem" (sometimes the same thought was expressed about the Suez Canal as well); and that after Israeli withdrawal the possibility could be discussed of a document that might be filed with the Secretary General, or of a Security Council resolution, that would finally end any possibility of claiming that a "state of belligerency" existed between Israel and her neighbors.

The Israeli position was that the Arab governments had repudiated the Armistice Agreements of 1949 by going to war; that the parties should meet alone, and draw up a treaty of peace; and that until negotiations for that purpose began, Israel would not weaken its bargaining position by publicly revealing its peace aims, although the Prime Minister and the Foreign Minister did state publicly and officially that Israel had no territorial claims as such, but was interested in the territorial problem only insofar as issues of security and maritime rights, and, of course, the problem of Jerusalem, were concerned. Meanwhile, Israel began its administration of Jerusalem, the West Bank, the Golan Heights, the Gaza Strip and Sinai as the occupying Power under the Cease-Fire Resolutions, justifying its policies "at the municipal level," and without annexations, in the perspective of that branch of international law.[2]

---

[1] See, *e.g.*, UN Doc. S/PV.1351, pp. 21-27, June 8, 1967.

[2] Stone, No Peace—No War in the Middle East 7-20 (1969); E. Lauterpacht, Jerusalem and the Holy Places 50-51 (1968); McNair and Watts, The Legal Effects of War, Ch. 17 (1966); Gutteridge, "The Protection of Civilians in Occupied Territory," The Yearbook of World Affairs 290 (1951); Stone, The Middle-East under Cease Fire 10-13 (1967); Gazit, Israel's Policy in the Administered

The United States, Canada, most of the West European and Latin American nations, and a large number of nations from other parts of the world supported a different approach, which ultimately prevailed.

In view of the taut circumstances of May and June, 1967, no majority could be obtained, either in the Security Council or the General Assembly, to declare Israel the aggressor. The question of who fired the first shot, difficult enough to resolve in itself, had to be examined as part of a sequence of Byzantine complexity: the false reports of Israeli mobilization against Syria; the removal of UNEF forces from the Sinai and the Gaza Strip; the closing of the Strait of Tiran; the mobilization of Arab forces around Israel, and the establishment of a unified command; and the cycle of statements, propaganda, speeches and diplomatic efforts which marked the final weeks before June 5. Before that mystery, sober opinion refused to reach the conclusion that Israel was the aggressor. No serious attempt was made to obtain a resolution declaring the United Arab Republic to be the aggressor.

Secondly, the majority opinion both in the General Assembly and in the Security Council supported the American view, first announced on June 5, 1967,[1] and stated more fully on June 19, 1967,[2] that after twenty bitter and tragic years of "war," "belligerency," and guerrilla activity in the Middle East, the quarrel had become a burden to world peace, and that the world community should finally insist on the establishment of a condition of peace, flowing from the agreement of the parties.

Third, the experience of the international community with the understandings which ended the Suez Crisis of

---

Territories (1969); Government of Israel, Two Years of Military Government, 1967-1969, (1969).

[1]   56 Dept. of State Bulletin 949-953 (1967).

[2]   President Johnson, "Principles for Peace in the Middle East," 57 Dept. of State Bulletin 31 (1967).

1956-1957 led to the conclusion that Israel should not be required to withdraw from the cease-fire lines except as part of a firm prior agreement which dealt with all the major issues in the controversy: justice for the refugees; guarantees of security for Israel's border, and her maritime rights in the Gulf of Aqaba and the Suez Canal; a solution for Jerusalem which met the legitimate interests of Jordan and of Israel, and of the three world religions which regard Jerusalem as a Holy City; and the establishment of a condition of peace.

In 1957, in deference to Arab sensitivity about seeming publicly to "recognize" Israel, to "negotiate" with Israel, or to make "peace" with Israel, the United States took the lead in negotiating understandings which led to the withdrawal of Israeli troops from the Sinai and the stationing of UNEF forces along the Sinai border, in the Gaza Strip, and at Sharm-el-Sheikh. The terms of that understanding were spelled out in a carefully planned series of statements made by the governments both in their capitals, and before the General Assembly. Egyptian commitments of the period were broken one by one, the last being the request for the removal of UNEF, and the closing of the Strait of Tiran to Israeli shipping in May, 1967. That step, it was clear from the international understandings of 1957, justified Israeli military action under Article 51 as an act of self-defense.[1]

Fourth, while the majority approach always linked Israeli withdrawal to the establishment of a condition of peace through an agreement among the parties which

---

[1] Many of the critical documents appear in Department of State, United States Policy in the Middle East, September, 1956-June, 1957 (1957, esp. pp. 332-342; United States Congress, Senate Committee on Foreign Relations, "A Select Chronology and Background Documents Relating to the Middle East," prepared by the Library of Congress, Legislative Reference Service (1967, rev. ed., 1969). See also H. Finer, Dulles over Suez (1964), Chs. 17 and 18.

would also resolve long-standing controversies about the refugees, maritime rights, and Jerusalem, the question remained, "To what boundaries should Israel withdraw?" On this issue, the American position was sharply drawn, and rested on a critical provision of the Armistice Agreements of 1949. Those agreements provided in each case that the Armistice Demarcation Line "is not to be construed in any sense as a political or territorial boundary, and is delineated without prejudice to rights, claims or positions of either Party to the Armistice as regards ultimate settlement of the Palestine question."[1] Many other provisions of each Agreement make it clear that the purpose of the Armistice was "to facilitate the transition from the present truce to permanent peace in Palestine" and that all such non-military "rights, claims, or interests" were subject to "later settlement" by agreement of the parties, as part of the transition from armistice to peace.[2] These paragraphs, which were put into the agreements at Arab insistence, were the legal foundation for the controversies over the wording of paragraphs 1 and 3 of Security Council Resolution 242, of November 22, 1967.[3]

---

[1] 42 UN Treaty Series, 256, Art. V, par. 2 (1949).

[2] *ibid.*, Preamble, p. 252; Art. I, p. 252; Art. IV, par. 3, p. 256; Art. XI and Art. XII, p. 268.

[3] The Security Council...(1) Affirms that the fulfillment of Charter principles requires the establishment of a just and lasting peace in the Middle East which should include the application of both the following principles:

(i) Withdrawal of Israeli armed forces from territories occupied in the recent conflict;

(ii) Termination of all claims or states of belligerency and respect for and acknowledgment of the sovereignty, territorial integrity and political independence of every State in the area and their

That resolution, promulgated under Chapter VI of the Charter, finally received the unanimous support of the Council. It was backed in advance by the assurance of the key countries that they would accept the resolution and work with Ambassador Jarring to implement it.

It is important to recall what the resolution requires. It calls upon the parties to reach "a peaceful and accepted" agreement which would definitively settle the Arab-Israeli controversy, and establish conditions of "just and lasting peace" in the area in accordance with the "provisions and principles" stated in the resolution. The agreement required by paragraph 3 of the resolution, the Security Council said, should establish "secure and recognized boundaries" between Israel and its neighbors "free from threats or acts of force," to replace the Armistice Demarcation Lines established in 1949, and the cease-fire lines of June, 1967. The Israeli armed forces should withdraw to such lines, as part of a comprehensive agreement, settling all the issues mentioned in the resolution, and in a condition of peace.

On this point, the American position has been the same under both the Johnson and the Nixon administrations. The new and definitive political boundaries should not represent "the weight of conquest," both administrations have said; on the other hand, under the policy and

---

right to live in peace within secure and recognized boundaries free from threats or acts of force;

(2) Affirms further the necessity

(a) For guaranteeing freedom of navigation through international waterways in the area;

(b) For achieving a just settlement of the refugee problem;

(c) For guaranteeing the territorial inviolability and political independence of every State in the area, through measures including the establishment of demilitarized zones.

language of the Armistice Agreements of 1949, and of the Security Council Resolution of November 22, 1967, they need not be the same as the Armistice Demarcation Lines.[1] The walls and machine guns that divided Jerusalem need not be restored. And adjustments can be made by agreement, under paragraph 2 of Security Council Resolution 242, to guarantee maritime rights "through international waterways in the area," and, equally, to guarantee "the territorial inviolability and political independence of every State in the area, through measures including the establishment of demilitarized zones."[2]

This is the legal significance of the omission of the word "the" from paragraph 1 (i) of the resolution, which calls for the withdrawal of Israeli armed forces "from territories occupied in the recent conflict," and not "from *the* territories occupied in the recent conflict." Repeated attempts to amend this sentence by inserting the word "the" failed in the Security Council. It is therefore not legally possible to assert that the provision requires Israeli withdrawal from *all* the territories now occupied under the Cease-Fire Resolutions to the Armistice Demarcation Lines.

This aspect of the relationship between the Security Council Resolution of November 22, 1967, and the Armistice Agreements of 1949 likewise explains the reference in the resolution to the rather murky principle of "the inadmissibility of the acquisition of territory by war." Whatever the full implications of that obscure idea may be, it would clearly permit the territorial adjustments and special security provisions called for by the Security Council resolution and the Armistice Agreements of 1949.

The resolution provided that the Secretary General should appoint a representative to consult with the

---

[1] Speech by President Johnson, Sept. 10, 1968, 59 Dept. of State Bulletin 348 (1968); Speech by Secretary Rogers, Dec. 9, 1969, 62 Dept. of State Bulletin 7 (1970).

[2] See note 1 on page 140.

parties, and assist them in reaching the agreement required by paragraph 3 of the resolution.

WHAT WEIGHT TO CONQUEST?

STEPHEN M. SCHWEBEL[1]

(EXCERPTS)

In his admirable address of December 9, 1969, on the situation in the Middle East, Secretary of State William P. Rogers took two positions of particular international legal interest, one implicit and the other explicit.[2] Secretary Rogers called upon the Arab states and Israel to establish "a state of peace... instead of the state of belligerency, which has characterized relations for over 20 years." Applying this and other elements of the American approach to the United Arab Republic and Israel, the Secretary of State suggested that, "in the context of peace and agreement [between the UAR and Israel] on specific

---

[1] Reprinted with permission from Stephen M. Schwebel, "What Weight to Conquest?" 64 AJIL 344 (1970), © The American Society of International Law. When this article appeared in 1970, Mr. Schwebel was Executive Director of the American Society of International Law and a Consultant on International Law to the Department of State. Since 1981, he has served on the International Court of Justice.

[2] The text is published in full in the New York Times, Dec. 11, 1969, p. 16.

security safeguards, withdrawal of Israeli forces from Egyptian territory would be required."[1]

Secretary Rogers accordingly inferred that, in the absence of such peace and agreement, withdrawal of Israeli forces from Egyptian territory would not be required. That is to say, he appeared to uphold the legality of continued Israeli occupation of Arab territory pending "the establishment of a state of peace between the parties instead of the state of belligerency..."[2] In this Secretary Rogers is on sound ground. That ground may well be based on appreciation of the fact that Israel's action in 1967 was defensive, and on the theory that, since the danger in response to which defensive action was taken remains, occupation—though not annexation—is justified, pending a peace settlement. But Mr. Rogers' conclusion may be simply a pragmatic judgment (indeed, certain other permanent members of the Security Council, which are not likely to share the foregoing legal perception, are not now pressing for Israeli withdrawal except as an element of a settlement).

More questionable, however, is the Secretary of State's explicit conclusion on a key question of the law and politics of the Middle East dispute: that "any changes in the preexisting [1949 armistice] lines should not reflect the weight of conquest and should be confined to insubstantial alterations required for mutual security. We do not support expansionism." Secretary Rogers referred approvingly in this regard to the Security Council's resolution of November, 1967, which,

---

[1] *Ibid.*

[2] *Ibid.*

Emphasizing the inadmissibility of the acquisition of territory by war[1] and the need to work for a just and lasting peace in which every State in the area can live in security,

Emphasizing further that all Member States in their acceptance of the Charter of the United Nations have undertaken a commitment to act in accordance with Article 2 of the Charter.

1. Affirms that the fulfillment of Charter principles requires the establishment of a just and lasting peace in the Middle East which should include the application of both the following principles:

(i) Withdrawal of Israeli armed forces from territories occupied in the recent conflict,[2]

(ii) Termination of all claims or states of belligerency and respect for and acknowledgment of the sovereignty, territorial integrity and political independence of every State in the area and their right to live in peace

---

[1] The resolution's use of the word "war" is of interest. The June, 1967, hostilities were not marked by a declaration of war. Certain Arab states have regarded themselves at war with Israel—or, at any rate, in a state of belligerency—since 1948, a questionable position under the law of the Charter. In view of the defeat in the United Nations organs of resolutions holding Israel to have been the aggressor in 1967, presumably the use of the word "war" was not meant to indicate that Israel's action was not in exercise of self-defense. It may be added that territory would not in any event be acquired by war, but, if at all, by the force of treaties of peace.

[2] It should be noted that the resolution does not specify "all territories" or "the territories" but "territories." The subparagraph immediately following is, by way of contrast, more comprehensively cast, specifying "all claims or states of belligerency."

within secure and recognized boundaries free from threats or acts of force...[1]

It is submitted that the Secretary's conclusion is open to question on two grounds: first, that it fails to distinguish between aggressive conquest and defensive conquest; second, that it fails to distinguish between the taking of territory which the prior holder held lawfully and that which it held unlawfully. These contentions share common ground.

As a general principle of international law, as that law has been reformed since the League, particularly by the Charter, it is both vital and correct to say that there shall be no weight to conquest, that the acquisition of territory by war is inadmissible.[2] But that principle must be read in particular cases together with other general principles, among them the still more general principle of which it is an application, namely, that no legal right shall spring from a wrong, and the Charter principle that the Members of the United Nations shall refrain in their international relations from the threat or use of force against the

---

[1] Res. 242 (1967) of Nov. 22, 1967; 62 AJIL 482 (1968). President Johnson, in an address of Sept. 10, 1968, declared:

"We are not the ones to say where other nations should draw the lines between them that will assure each the greatest security. It is clear, however, that a return to the situation of June 4, 1967, will not bring peace. There must be secure and there must be recognized borders...

"At the same time, it should be equally clear that boundaries cannot and should not reflect the weight of conquest. Each change must have a reason which each side, in honest negotiation, can accept as part of a just compromise." (59 Department of State Bulletin 348 (1968).)

[2] See, however, Kelsen, Principles of International Law 420-433 (2nd ed. by Tucker, 1967).

territorial integrity or political independence of any state. So read, the distinctions between aggressive conquest and defensive conquest, between the taking of territory legally held and the taking of territory illegally held, become no less vital and correct than the central principle itself.

Those distinctions may be summarized as follows: (a) A state acting in lawful exercise of its right of self-defense may seize and occupy foreign territory as long as such seizure and occupation are necessary to its self-defense. (b) As a condition of its withdrawal from such territory, that state may require the institution of security measures reasonably designed to ensure that that territory shall not again be used to mount a threat or use of force against it of such a nature as to justify exercise of self-defense. (c) Where the prior holder of territory had seized that territory unlawfully, the state which subsequently takes that territory in the lawful exercise of self-defense has, against that prior holder, better title.

The facts of the June, 1967, "Six Day War" demonstrate that Israel reacted defensively against the threat and use of force against her by her Arab neighbors This is indicated by the fact that Israel responded to Egypt's prior closure of the Straits of Tiran, its proclamation of a blockade of the Israeli port of Elath [sic], and the manifest threat of the UAR's use of force inherent in its massing of troops in Sinai, coupled with its ejection of UNEF. It is indicated by the fact that, upon Israeli responsive action against the UAR, Jordan initiated hostilities against Israel. It is suggested as well by the fact that, despite the most intense efforts by the Arab states and their supporters, led by the Premier of the Soviet Union, to gain condemnation of Israel as an aggressor by the hospitable organs of the United Nations, those efforts were decisively defeated. The conclusion to which these facts lead is that the Israeli conquest of Arab and Arab-held territory was defensive rather than aggressive conquest.

The facts of the 1948 hostilities between the Arab invaders of Palestine and the nascent state of Israel further demonstrate that Egypt's seizure of the Gaza strip, and Jordan's seizure and subsequent annexation of the West Bank and the old city of Jerusalem, were unlawful. Israel was proclaimed to be an independent state within the boundaries allotted to her by the General Assembly's partition resolution. The Arabs of Palestine and of neighboring Arab states rejected that resolution. But that rejection was no warrant for the invasion by those Arab states of Palestine, whether of territory allotted to Israel, to the projected, stillborn Arab state or to the projected, internationalized city of Jerusalem. It was no warrant for attack by the armed forces of neighboring Arab states upon the Jews of Palestine, whether they resided within or without Israel. But that attack did justify Israeli defensive measures, both within and, as necessary, without the boundaries allotted her by the partition plan (as in the new city of Jerusalem). It follows that the Egyptian occupation of Gaza, and the Jordanian annexation of the West Bank and Jerusalem, could not vest in Egypt and Jordan lawful, indefinite control, whether as occupying Power or sovereign: *ex injuria jus non oritur*.

If the foregoing conclusions that (a) Israeli action in 1967 was defensive and (b) Arab action in 1948, being aggressive, was inadequate to legalize Egyptian and Jordanian taking of Palestinian territory, are correct, what follows?

It follows that the application of the doctrine of according no weight to conquest requires modification in double measure. In the first place, having regard to the consideration that, as between Israel acting defensively in 1948 and 1967, on the one hand, and her Arab neighbors, acting aggressively in 1948 and 1967, on the other, Israel has better title in the territory of what was Palestine, including the whole of Jerusalem, than do Jordan and Egypt (the UAR indeed has, unlike Jordan, not asserted sovereign title), it follows that modifications of the 1949 armistice lines among those states within former Palestinian territory are lawful (if not necessarily desirable), whether those modifications are, in Secretary Rogers' words, "insubstantial alterations required for mutual security" or more substantial alterations—such as recognition of Israeli sovereignty over the whole of Jerusalem.[1] In the second place, as regards territory bordering Palestine, and under unquestioned Arab sovereignty in 1949 and thereafter, such as Sinai and the Golan Heights, it follows not that no weight shall be given to conquest, but that such weight shall be given to defensive action as is reasonably required to ensure that such Arab territory will not again be used for aggressive purposes against Israel. For example—and this appears to be envisaged both by the Secretary of State's address and the resolution of the Security Council—free navigation through the Straits of Tiran shall be effectively guaranteed and demilitarized zones shall be established.

The foregoing analysis accords not only with the terms of the United Nations Charter, notably Article 2, paragraph 4, and Article 51, but law and practice as they have developed since the Charter's conclusion. In point of practice, it is instructive to recall that the Republic of Korea and indeed the United Nations itself have given considerable weight to conquest in Korea, to the extent of that substantial territory north of the 38th parallel from which the aggressor was driven and remains excluded—a territory which, if the full will of the United Nations had prevailed, would have been much larger (indeed, perhaps the whole of North Korea). In point of law, provisions of the Vienna Convention on the Law of Treaties are pertinent. Article 52 provides that "A treaty is void if its conclusion has been procured by the threat or use of force in violation of the principles of international law embodied in the Charter of the United Nations"—a provision which clearly does not debar conclusion of a treaty where force has been applied, as in self-defense, in accordance with the

---

[1] It should be added that the armistice agreements of 1949 expressly preserved the territorial claims of all parties and did not purport to establish definitive boundaries between them.

Charter. And Article 75 provides that "The provisions of the present Convention are without prejudice to any obligation in relation to a treaty which may arise for an aggressor State in consequence of measures taken in conformity with the Charter of the United Nations with reference to that State's aggression."

The state of the law has been correctly summarized by Elihu Lauterpacht, who points out that

> territorial change cannot properly take place as a result of the unlawful use of force But to omit the word "unlawful" is to change the substantive content of the rule and to turn an important safeguard of legal principle into an aggressor's charter. For if force can never be used to effect lawful territorial chance, then, if territory has once changed hands as a result of the unlawful use of force, the illegitimacy of the position thus established is sterilized by the prohibition upon the use of force to restore the lawful sovereign. This cannot be regarded as reasonable or correct.[1]

---

[1] Elihu Lauterpacht, Jerusalem and the Holy Places, Anglo-Israel Association, Pamphlet No. 19 (1968), p. 52.